> Carter,
> Thanks for your interest in my work. You have a role in what must be done.
> I hope you enjoy my book.
> Dwyt

PROPERLY UNDERSTOOD

If Citizens Are To Be Free

DWIGHT YODER

Copyrighted Material

Properly Understood
Copyright © 2023 by Dwight Yoder. All Rights Reserved.
No part of this publication may be reproduced, stored in a retrieval system, or transmitted in any form or by any means—electronic, mechanical, photocopying, recording, or otherwise—without prior written permission from the publisher, except for the inclusion of brief quotations in a review.

Published by Praxeology Forum

979-8-9871460-0-2 (print)
979-8-9871460-1-9 (eBook)

Cover and Interior design: 1106 Design

CONTENTS

Introduction 1

Part I
Fundamental Principles True for All Times.................. 11
    Human Nature... 13
    Human Action... 21
    Worldview.. 29
    Economics.. 37
    Knowledge, Tools, Science 47
    Power and Freedom...................................... 59
    Belief Systems... 73

Part II
Analysis and Synthesis 81
    Thinking Like a Ruler.................................. 83
    Feedback, Self-correcting, Distortion.................. 89
    Information Structure.................................. 101
    Economic Structure..................................... 115
    Social Structure 129
    Monetary and Financial Structure 145
    Rulership Structure.................................... 167

Part III
Structural Basis of Inequality 181
    Inequality 183
    Education 197
    Economic System. 223

Part IV
Going Forward 235
    Don't Just "Do Something" 237
    Competing Worldviews 247
    Responsibility and Feedback 257
    Transition 267

Conclusion. 273
Acknowledgements 283
Index 285

INTRODUCTION

*"There are a thousand hacking at the branches of evil
to one who is striking at the root . . . "*
Henry David Thoreau

*"The majority of them believe that a man will be led to do what is just
and good by following his own interest rightly understood."*
Alexis de Tocqueville

Sometimes we know things are not working. Our challenges with inequality, education, medical care, retirement, economic growth, and so on continue to worsen rather than improve. We work harder and harder, trying one technique after another, and yet get no closer to our goal or no closer to solving our problem. At some point, we must question whether we are on the right path. Perhaps we need to work backward and find a critical junction at which we could have taken a more productive turn. In other cases, we need to reevaluate our goal or reframe our problem. If our goal or problem is big and complicated, we may take a path for decades before we see clearly that "we can't get there from here." We are at such a junction today. Recognizing that we are on the wrong path is the starting point, the necessary requirement, for pausing and figuring out what is required to build a desirable future.

When decades of working harder and spending more money not only fail to resolve problems but makes them worse, citizens will respond and society will begin to change. When these realizations happen at times of increasing stress due to internal problems and external events, citizens may respond in ways that create an unstable society.

Frustration and contention will increase steadily, ultimately moving the mood of society toward emotional responses in place of objective analyses. The next stage in the progression is the development of a psychological state which various thinkers have described as regression, alienation, and anomie. This is a harmful state in which citizens distrust each other, groups polarize intransigently, and effective leadership becomes difficult, if not impossible. American society is well along this progression as evidenced, for example, by personal attacks, group conflict, censoring, street violence, and election-related violence. Because real solutions are not in view, each group is in a desperate race to gain power.

I believe that most citizens know that a race for power is not a sustainable solution, but it seems there are no viable alternatives. However, I claim there is a path to halt our current progression and restore a functioning society. It requires a return to the basics.

I wrote this book in response to our present challenges. It is based on work I began in the early 1990s when I was beginning to perceive that we might be on the wrong path, and seriously so. Since that time I have continuously adjusted my analysis and understanding based on observations of our society and elsewhere in the world. Until a few years ago, this work was simply my personal project, not a book-writing endeavor. Two things caused me to change my outlook and decide to publicly present my work. One of these was the increasing frequency and intensity of events which confirmed my assessments and analyses. The second and decisive change was my growing appreciation of the responsibility of each citizen to help find the right path. Thus, this book is my contribution to our collective effort—a message from one citizen to his fellow citizens.

This is not a book arguing for or against the policies of a particular political party. It does not propose a set of simple solutions for each of our particular problems. On the contrary, I explain why party-specific policies directed at specific problems are not working and cannot work. One reason people are frustrated is that after several decades of attempting to solve problems one at a time using previous methods, the problems are becoming more severe rather than improving. The purpose of this book is to show that alternative perspectives, proper understanding, and a reframing of our problems is required to obtain real and sustainable solutions.

We need to recognize and accept that our social and political climate is new. It is not just another cycle of American politics.

It is true that since our founding, American politics has been contentious: strong disagreement is part of our heritage. Today, however, healthy disagreement has turned into unhealthy conflict. Rather than turning to persuasion and tolerance, we increasingly turn to coercion, censorship, and suppression of free speech. Instead of respect and patience, we more easily vilify, condemn, and hold in contempt those who disagree with us. In place of compromise and respect for the democratic process, we grow impatient and are more willing to defeat or overpower those who disagree with us. Examples of where this shows up today include racism, economic inequality, marriage and family, pronoun usage, personal responsibility, and traditional religion.

The intensity of disagreement has brought about anger among groups and, in some cases, outright contempt of one group for another, and contempt kills relationships. While social pressures have been building for decades, clear and obvious manifestations of our failed attempts and of our dysfunctional emotional climate are recent. A critical question is, how did this come to be? First, we recognize that strong social conflict—the kind of conflict that is dangerous to a society—is fueled when people perceive that important values and freedoms are being threatened and especially when people fear they will be coerced to act in ways that violate those values and freedoms. With that acknowledgement, the question then becomes, why and how did we get to a situation in which some groups feel threatened and coerced by other groups? I offer an explanation that is different from the prevailing debates.

At the time of this writing, our public discussion focuses much more on what is wrong and what divides us rather than on what is good and what unites us. Fortunately, a large majority of Americans do broadly agree on many important issues and do share common values. I will point out these positive things throughout the book. I believe these shared values are one reason for optimism. The second reason is that citizens of the United States are truly free to vote at the ballot box. We are not prevented from voting by the military nor forced to vote a certain way out of fear. We are also free to vote socially and economically in ways that will be discussed later. This freedom to vote is the only foundation on which solutions can be developed. It is a source of great optimism but also of great challenge because it places responsibility on us.

Because we have this freedom and because it is the basis for restoring our society, a central subject of this book is the roles and responsibilities of each individual citizen. A country must do two things if it wishes to maintain and improve its way of life. First, it must defend itself from enemies. Second, it must function internally in ways that meet the expectations of most people within the country. The likelihood that these two conditions will be met depends on the quality of the rulership. This is true regardless of the form of rulership, whether it be monarchy, oligarchy, or democracy. If the rulership consistently fails, it is likely to be replaced by a foreign power or replaced through revolution, coup, or election. Therefore, it is of utmost importance to understand how this principle operates in a modern democratic republic.

A democracy is unique because those who are ruled—that is, all citizens—directly select their rulers. Thus, the people ultimately decide the quality of their rulers. Given the principle presented earlier regarding rulership, it is clear that the protection and flourishing of a democratic society depends on the ability of the citizenry to select rulers and hold them accountable. If the citizenry fails in those tasks, their society will be at risk in the same ways as if the king in a monarchical society were to turn despotic or become incompetent.

What might such a failure by citizens look like for the United States? Within a democracy, what is analogous to a despotic king? It is for the people to support coercion rather than democratic ideals. This coercion may be clear and explicit or it may be partially cloaked in the formality of democratic processes. Venezuela provides a current example in which it is easy to see the process and consequences of the clear and explicit choices made by its citizens. In 1998, because the people of Venezuela had become impatient and dissatisfied with democracy as practiced in their country, they voted to give power to the socialist dictator Hugo Chavez. Today, the country is in ruin, and the people have suffered greatly. This happened because a majority of the citizens did not understand what was happening or what they were doing. Some Americans believe that this could never happen here, while others, observing recent election cycles, believe we have already demonstrated that it is possible.

The more likely way in which "despotic" failure would take place in the United States is that it would be cloaked in the democratic process. The citizens of a democracy must be committed to democratic ideals, one of the most important of which is protecting the minority from the majority. Many who have studied democracy over the centuries have recognized the threat of "tyranny of the majority." As respect for this principle of protecting minority interests decreases, the contest for political power will become more intense, more divisive, and ultimately more ruthless. A democracy cannot survive if such a process continues. The society will break down in some way. Elections and political activity of recent years have made clear that the United States has begun this process. However, I believe that we are in the early stages and have time to reverse course.

In what follows, I use *incompetence* in the purely objective meaning of repeated failure to make decisions which are good for society. Consider the example of a kingdom. Incompetence does not necessarily mean that the king no longer cares about his subjects nor that he is mentally deficient. In fact, the king and his court may be working hard and doing their very best, but circumstances have overwhelmed them. No matter how hard the king tries, if his decisions repeatedly result in unsolved problems and in creating undesirable circumstances, the kingdom will continue to suffer until a disruptive change occurs.

In a democracy, we may speak of incompetent government leaders, but ultimately the necessary competence must be possessed by citizens because only citizens have the power to select and remove rulers. Citizens make decisions by voting electorally, economically, and socially. If they get overwhelmed or get on the wrong path for any reason and cast their votes incompetently—that is, in ways that do not produce desirable results—the society will suffer and, if poor voting continues long enough, the society will be transformed into a society with less freedom, or in the extreme case will be defeated in some manner.

In the United States, a probable form of this transformation or defeat is that a ruling class will seize power and will not be accountable to the citizens, although formal democratic processes will continue so as to give the illusion of freedom. One of the primary goals of this book is to explain how the United States came to be in a situation which made it difficult for citizens to make competent decisions. There is good news, however: it is not too late.

The title of this book comes from the work of Alexis de Tocqueville, who published *Democracy in America* in 1835, a mere fifty years after our Constitution was ratified. He had great insight and foresight about the nature of society and government in the young United States. One of his observations was that the success of the country, up to that time and for the future, depended on the "self-interest properly understood" of the citizenry.

"We the people" means all Americans, past, present, and future. No generation stands alone. We the people, past and present, are responsible for our present reality, for that which is good and that which needs improvement, and for that which poses a problem. We the people, present, are responsible for what we do with our existing reality, both for our benefit and for future citizens. While those statements of fact may be easy to accept in the abstract, they can be disconcerting when considered closely. When we place the blame on politicians in Washington or on big business or on our educational system or on immigration, and so on, we must accept that we the people collectively caused or allowed all of those things to come about. At present, the levels of concern, of divisiveness, of frustration, and of anger are higher than most Americans can recall. In the midst of this, "we the people" must ask how we let this happen. As I will show throughout this book, everything that exists today, and the form in which it exists, is the result of many decisions made by many citizens over many years.

The key to finding solutions for our current problems and preparing for a better future is to interpret those many decisions using a changed perspective, a proper understanding, and a new framework so that we can make better decisions going forward.

How we make decisions about our behavior and how we modify those decisions based on experience will be discussed throughout the book. As we move through life, we follow these basic steps: we think and plan, we act, we observe results, we think about those results in order to decide if we should modify our behavior, we respond accordingly. I will show how particular circumstances, perspectives, and understanding, which have developed from the end of World War II until the present, have created an environment in which it was easy to be misled by the results of our actions and by our interpretation of the results. Because we were misled, we made decisions—that is, we voted in various ways—which brought about what we experience today.

We must return to the basics if we are to develop new perspectives and proper understanding, and to reframe our problems. This reworking is necessary so that we can first begin unwinding our psychological state. This unwinding is a prerequisite for finding solutions to our reframed problems. A key element of a new perspective is that an integrated, broad understanding and approach is needed. We cannot make progress by attempting to fix things one at a time. Furthermore, to develop an integrated understanding requires an ordered presentation of ideas and information that are systematically linked together.

The first part of the book covers fundamental principles which are relevant to any society at any time. They are timeless, showing up through 5,000 years of recorded history across cultures and civilizations. Although different societies have understood and manifested these concepts differently, certain core elements show up consistently. They can be stated in general terms and accepted as principles. When a society forgets these principles or orders itself as if they are not true, the society will suffer. Because they are fundamental principles, we must grasp them as the first step in reordering our thinking.

Each of the subjects in Part One is a major field in itself and has been studied for hundreds, if not thousands, of years. I will address only those elements from each field which are needed for the purposes of this book and will do so in the simplest manner suitable for conveying the essential fact or principle.

The fundamental principles serve as the background building blocks upon which each society or civilization develops given the characteristics of its time. Each historical time is different from others but is always subject to the fundamental principles. At each time in the life of a society or civilization, what exists is not only a reflection of its history but, in fact, embodies its history. Therefore, each chapter in Part One contains a second section discussing the principles in question in terms of the present characteristics of our society.

Building upon the first part, the second part of the book offers an analysis and synthesis of the function and structure of our society.

Because *inequality* is the term most commonly used today to speak about many of our social problems, Part Three of the book considers this subject in detail.

Finally, the fourth and last part will bring everything together and present ideas for going forward. That is, I will offer my thinking about how we use our updated perspectives, understanding, and reframing to begin changing how we think and operate as citizens.

Early in this project of presenting an integrated view of broad scope, I faced the decision of how to simplify. Many entire books have been written about each subject I needed to address. My decision was for brevity versus a more representative treatment. The latter would have resulted in a much longer book and would likely have reduced clarity. Since brevity won, I've included only those points most essential to achieving the purpose of this book.

For the same reasons, I will only include direct references to other works when to do otherwise would seem inappropriate. Much of what I say in this book is my synthesis of what has been said by multiple people throughout history. When I directly use an idea or material that is easily attributed to a major source, I will reference it. An important clarification: when another person is quoted or referenced, it does not mean that I am in full agreement with all of their work; it simply means that the particular point is useful or illuminating for the present discussion.

Part I

FUNDAMENTAL PRINCIPLES TRUE FOR ALL TIMES

"... a frequent recurrence to fundamental principles ... is absolutely necessary to preserve the blessings of liberty and keep a government free."
Benjamin Franklin

"One of the most dangerous errors instilled into us by 19th century progressive optimism is the idea that civilization is automatically bound to increase and spread. The lesson of history is the opposite; civilization is a rarity, attained with difficulty and easily lost."
C. S. Lewis

HUMAN NATURE

"In each of us, two natures are at war—the good and the evil. All our lives the fight goes on between them, and one of them must conquer."
Robert Louis Stevenson

"Why has government been instituted at all? Because the passions of man will not conform to the dictates of reason and justice without constraint."
Alexander Hamilton

The Principles

What we understand and believe about human nature shapes how we understand everything else. Human nature is the set of characteristics common to humankind and includes physical, intellectual, psychological, and social aspects. What is common is not, of course, the details of our actions but rather our general tendencies, behaviors, and traits. As will be true for every subject, we will look only at aspects which are necessary for the purposes of this book.

Human nature refers to innate characteristics, sometimes called natural or basic characteristics, not to a description of how a particular person succeeds or fails within their society. As a simple example, human height is a natural attribute which, within an environment, is largely determined by genetics and thus falls within human nature. However, whether that person becomes a star basketball player does not belong to the concept of human nature because the choice of a profession is determined by many factors extrinsic to human nature as such.

Appreciating the differences and variability of traits among people is essential in understanding how society functions—both the benefits and the problems. Throughout the book we will use the explanatory power that comes from understanding human variability.

The variability of natural traits measured across a population can often be approximated by a bell curve. Bell curves are commonly explained by using human height as an example. If the heights of a group of people are measured and plotted, the plot will show that the largest percentage of people have an average height. The curve will also be symmetric, with as many people being taller than average as there are people who are shorter than average. The shape of the curve (which looks like a bell) will show that a large majority of people have a height within several inches of either side of the average. The "tails" of the curve will show that a very small percentage of people are exceptionally short or tall. As we will see, the fact that natural characteristics follow a bell curve and therefore exhibit the above properties turns out to be useful in understanding and communicating much of what we observe in society.

Temperament and personality are particularly important. People are born with certain tendencies and capabilities which interact with their developmental environment to produce various traits, most of which follow a bell curve distribution. Personality traits, physical capacities, and intelligence are some of the characteristics important for studying social function.

People have always socialized, formed groups, and even created civilizations. Hierarchy is a necessary part of that organizing impulse. A rulership or power structure always develops. How this structure comes about, how it operates, and how it is justified differ depending on the historical context but is always the dominant force in a society. A society without structure is not possible, and a society without an effective and justified structure will fail.

All written historical records reveal that societies possess a sense of morality, of right and wrong, of good and bad. Across time and geography there is significant commonality when it comes to the basics of moral codes. A desire for fairness and justice seems to be innate, and prohibitions against violence and theft are universal. Although there are common concepts among moral codes, the particular details vary by society.

A moral code must be taught and enforced. Therefore, every society is intentional about teaching (passing along) moral expectations to the next generation. Nonetheless, because of human nature there will forever be some individuals who will disrupt society by violating the law. As a result, every law code stipulates punishments for violating the law. So, we see that the need for a law code, the need for development of right behavior, and the need for punishment of offenders all arise from human nature.

Like moral codes, religion (or a belief system) is as old as humanity, with evidence predating written records. Although the practices and content of religions have differed, every society has possessed a religion. Belief systems shape cultures, drive civilizations, and inspire conflict. Belief systems provide a basis for the *shoulds* and *should nots* for a society. In addition, religion provides some element of transcendence, the need for which is part of human nature.

Another constant characteristic of human nature is conflict within and among groups. The conflict may be fueled by greed, envy, love, pride, fear, or competition for resources, power, or esteem. Humans have a natural tendency to transfer anxiety and blame onto others. We also have a built-in drive to imitate others and to respond directly to what we observe in others. This explains the perpetual observation of mob behavior compared to what an individual will do on their own. These human characteristics work together to generate conflict. Within a social group the conflict may be between individuals or between subgroups. An "us versus them" mindset seems to develop naturally, especially under conditions of anxiety, uncertainty, or threat.

Conflict among subgroups, if it progresses far enough and if not crushed by a stronger power, will be resolved by the scapegoat mechanism or by civil war. Between separate societies, escalation leads to war. All of these forms of conflict are harmful to a society. One of the reasons for this harm is that the moral code is at times openly violated during "us versus them" conflicts. As a result, all cultures, societies, and civilizations create beliefs, rituals, and institutions to minimize the occurrence and harm of conflicts.

We are pattern-seeking and meaning-seeking beings. At the simplest level, those characteristics are essential for survival, perhaps more so in our primitive past than at present. At higher levels they represent aspects of our human nature that serve our need to understand and our desire to have a sense of control of our life and future. If a person cannot obtain a satisfactory sense of understanding and control, they will become anxious, and if it goes far enough, they will develop a disordered mind. If a sufficient number of people within a society get into that state, the society may become disordered.

In presenting the above aspects of human nature, it was relatively easy to make simple statements. However, dealing with human motivations, which are also part of our nature, is more complicated. The starting point is the fact that people act—they do things—in response to threats and desires. In thinking of human motivations, I've found Maslow's hierarchy of needs, or motivational hierarchy, to be useful. He represented his model in a six-level pyramid in which the lower levels take priority. (His original model had five levels, but he later discovered the need for a sixth level.) There is a progression up the pyramid when the previous level has been met at some degree of satisfaction. Threat, desire, and beliefs can produce powerful motivations at any level and may result in subjugation, coercion, and war.

The six levels are (1) physiological (what it takes to sustain life itself); (2) safety (security of self, resources, property); (3) love and belonging; (4) esteem (self-confidence, respect of others, achievement); (5) self-actualization (creativity, morality, problem-solving); and (6) self-transcendence. It is a useful model because it is simple, because the six categories do represent aspects of human nature, and because there is some degree of hierarchy in our development. For example, a person struggling to simply stay alive every day is not going to invest much time in studying philosophy or developing a theory of art. Of course, human behavior is not expressed in a strictly sequential manner. For example, evidence of art and music predates written history by thousands of years. Also, many practitioners of religions have a strong element of self-transcendence at the same time they are struggling to survive. I think of the levels as indicating where a person tends to invest incrementally available resources. The key point is that these motivating needs are part of human nature and are useful for understanding a society.

For some people, the most difficult thing to accept about human nature is that the basic elements and propensities do not change. However, the lessons from history make this clear. Law codes from more than 4,000 years ago talk about the same types of problems as do our current laws. History and literature confirm the same constancy. People have always had the capacity to do good and evil, and to act with virtue and vice. Although human nature has not changed, societies have experimented with different forms to moderate, influence, and control human behavior for the good of society. The quality of life in a society depends on its success in dealing with the good and bad within human nature—something we will explore throughout the book.

Present Characteristics

Although the basic elements of human nature don't change, the manifestation of the principles does vary depending on the particulars of a society. Much of how we understand human nature and how we express it today can be explained by three big trends which were well underway by 1700. These are philosophy, science, and prosperity. Because those three areas will show up throughout the book, in this chapter we only briefly note their influence relative to the principles discussed above.

(By *philosophy* I mean the ideas, ways of thinking, and the subjects that were part of philosophical study prior to the twentieth century. Today, much of the work in philosophy departments of universities is quite abstract, technical, and of a substantially different character than that of earlier centuries.)

The natural variability in traits among individuals exists as potential which can only be expressed under certain conditions. For example, a person with a mix of traits ideal for a speedskater will never realize that potential if they are born into a desert tribe isolated from the rest of the world. Similarly, a person who would be a great government administrator will have no opportunity to serve if the class rules for that society prevent their engagement in government. Our circumstances today provide freedom, capacities, and opportunities for the expression of an extremely wide range of attributes.

For most of the past 2,000 years, Christianity was the religion that shaped Europe and the United States, not only morally but socially and politically. Christianity's direct influence in Europe has steadily declined over the past 200 years and is now greatly reduced. The diminishing of the direct influence of Christianity in the United States is an active process and one that continues to generate social friction. Because human nature requires a belief system, the diminishment of Christianity means that other belief systems will fill any voids. In fact, this transition of belief systems is one of the important stories of our time.

Increasing prosperity brought dramatic improvements in material well-being to hundreds of millions of people. As a result, many people now have the option of moving up Maslow's pyramid of human motivations. That is, they can invest more resources in those levels beyond what is required for survival, safety, and basic relationships. Such a rapid change in potential for a large portion of the population is brand-new in history, with social, economic, and political implications that we are just beginning to understand.

Internationally, at least for the major world powers, conflict has moved from physical warfare to the arena of economic domination, which, of course, can degenerate into physical warfare. Conflict within countries is primarily driven by economic inequality and by a widening gap between the "ruling elites" and a large portion of the populace. This gap is both economic and cultural. At present, nothing is in view which might mitigate the forces behind both international and domestic conflicts. Without moderating influences, these conflicts will escalate until a crisis brings about some form of resolution.

Our world today presents challenges for our desire, indeed our need, for understanding and control. Our capacity for pattern matching and for discerning meaning are increasingly inadequate for the complexity, specialization, fragmentation, and pace of change we face. As a result, some citizens will see their place in society as incomprehensible and irrational. If such a state continues, it will lead to harm both for the individual and then for society.

Events of the first half of the twentieth century shattered any remaining hope that ideas based on reason, which were formed over the previous centuries, would produce ever more peaceful, free, and prosperous societies. Human nature was once again proved unchanging. This reality altered the intellectual underpinnings of Europe and set the stage for a reordering of the world following World War II. Broadly, two paths were taken from that point: democracy and communism. Today, it is clear that both of those paths have again confirmed human nature, which in turn has us again approaching a critical juncture.

HUMAN ACTION

"The most important single central fact about a free market is that no exchange takes place unless both parties benefit."
Milton Friedman

"The price of anything is the amount of life you exchange for it."
Henry David Thoreau

The Principles

Human nature is expressed through human action. The nature of society and the quality of life in a society are determined by the actions of people. Human action drives history. (Of course, events such as natural disasters—outside of human control—do happen, but in the end, humans must still respond to those external events.) Thus, it is essential to understand the principles underlying human action.

Human action is always individual. It is only the individual who has the capability to rationally decide when and how to act. We may speak of a group having acted. We might say "the government" or "business" or "the school board" has made a decision or taken some action. This does not mislead as long as we remember that it is a shorthand representation for the collective action of individual decisions. It is true that people acting as part of a group may make different decisions and may behave differently than they would individually, but the "group effect" is simply one of multiple influences affecting the individual.

We must make decisions about our actions because we live in a world with scarce resources and uncertainty. That is, we can't have everything we want in the quantity we want and at the time we want. We must make decisions and tradeoffs. This is true whether motivated by threat or desire and regardless of where we are operating on the scale of human motivations. Something must be given or risked in order to obtain the preferred state. Furthermore, the future is not known. The actions of other people or natural events can disrupt our plans. Thus, human action is a continuous activity requiring constant assessment and adjustment.

Prior to acting, a person must think about those things they may want to accomplish and must assess the required resources weighed against the likelihood of success. Stated more formally, at any time, a person has a set of *ends*: goals, objectives, things they want to be true. Each person also has a collection of *means*: knowledge, resources, information about risks, technology, opportunities. The individual will analyze the combinations to decide what *ends* will be pursued and what *means* will be used. The number of options may be few and simple for a person in a remote village in which all members struggle to survive. On the other hand, in modern societies, the options may be confusing in their number and complexity. Understanding *means*, though not simple, is more straightforward than is grasping the subtleties of *ends*. It is the latter which has the more profound social implications.

In the chapter on human nature, we used Maslow's hierarchy as a way to talk about the range of motivations for human action. In this chapter where we are talking specifically about such action, we can make some general observations. In general, if a person is acting in the lower levels of the motivational pyramid, more time and resources must be invested to meet the basic requirements of existence. Both the *ends* and *means* are easier to understand and decide upon. However, in the upper levels of the pyramid, the *ends* and *means* become much more difficult to assess. For example, if an individual is considering their desired status or social esteem or happiness twenty years in the future, there are multiple ends which they imagine might satisfy their motivations, but there is no way to know with certainty. Furthermore, if a specific end is chosen, there will be multiple means which could be imagined to be effective, but again with much uncertainty.

All means by which we act are, in their most essential nature, exchanges. For example, a person might exchange an hour of leisure time for an hour of labor in their garden in order to make it more productive or more beautiful. An hour of additional labor can be given in exchange for money which can then be exchanged for food or clothing. A military act may be exchanged for the protection of a society. Grasping that all human action involves an exchange is crucial for understanding all behavior but especially for those that impact society broadly.

Each person maintains a benefit scale by which to assess all potential exchanges. A benefit scale is not a formal, unchanging list but rather represents how a person ranks possible objectives at a given point in time under a given set of circumstances. Consider a simple example in which a person has one dollar and is going to decide from three options: 1) buy an apple, 2) buy an orange, 3) keep the dollar for some future use. The person will use their benefit scale to make the decision. If given the same options tomorrow, the decision might be different. The position of possible objectives on the benefit scale is one purely of ranking, one above or below another.

It can't be quantified to indicate that something is twice as desirable compared to something else. It is only possible to know the *ordering* of a person's benefit scale at a *point* in time by *observing* their actions. Reference to a benefit scale is the basis for all decisions regarding human action.

(A benefit scale is commonly called a value scale. I've chosen *benefit* to avoid confusion when talking about personal values in the moral sense.)

The well-being of an individual and of society depends on each citizen being effective in whatever role they play within the society. This requires people to have appropriately ranked *ends* as well as the necessary *means* to accomplish them. The development of *ends* and *means* and the necessary decision-making skills is influenced by the prevailing worldview, by training, by circumstances, and other factors, all of which will be considered in more detail in later chapters. A society will do well only if the vast majority of citizens make good decisions in choosing *ends* and using *means*.

Just as a person must learn how to act effectively, they must learn how to judge the actions of others. When we assess the actions of others, we need to be aware of two common errors.

First, all action is rational to the actor. A person acts based upon their benefit scale using the means they think most likely to succeed. Whether they are effective or whether they will eventually be satisfied is a different matter. To that individual, the action is rational because having assessed efficacy, cost, and risk, they think it is the best path to achieve some objective. When one person judges the actions of another to be irrational, it would usually be more accurate to say one of the following: 1) that the two individuals have benefit scales so different they appear incomprehensible or wrong to the other person, or 2) that the person whose action is being judged is using means the observer believes will certainly fail to achieve the objective.

If we believe another person is acting irrationally, rather than thinking more carefully about the situation, we may try to "fix" the other person, or we may try to force them to act in a way that we believe is rational. However, if we accept the behavior as rational and instead make assessments as noted in the paragraph above, our response will be different. Maybe the right response is to do nothing, that is, to be tolerant of differences. On the other hand, it may be that we can help the other person see the advantages of reshaping their benefit scale or of being trained to acquire more knowledge or skills to better achieve their goals.

A second common error has to do with fairness. A third-party, someone not part of an actual exchange, might judge the exchange between two other people to be unfair. But of course that judgment is based on the opinion of the third person. Suppose, for example, that a worker exchanges a day of labor for a loaf of bread. A third party might judge the conditions of the exchange as unfair. Perhaps the observing party thinks that two loaves would be more fair. Certainly, the idea of fairness is important in all relationships and therefore in society as a whole, but fairness is subjective. Later, we will look at the types of social problems that can occur when one group in society tries to enforce "fairness" upon the exchanges other people make.

When two individuals make an exchange, each of them did so because they thought the exchange would improve their circumstances. If I exchange one dollar for an apple, it is because at that moment I wanted an apple more than the dollar. Likewise, the person who owned the apple preferred to have the dollar. We did *not* exchange things of equal value, yet we sometimes hear a transaction described as involving things of equal value. This subtle error in thinking can be significant, especially when judging fairness in society.

A person must learn to be effective in human action. Some of this learning occurs naturally while growing up as a member in society. Other learning comes when one person intentionally trains another. Which actions are effective in a particular society is collectively learned over time through cause-effect feedback. Some actions result in progress toward a desired end, some are neutral, and some are counterproductive. People change actions and refine techniques as a result of this feedback. In a small, primitive society cause-effect connections are likely to be quick, whereas today the connections may be hard to discern.

Present Characteristics

Human action is a central characteristic of our age. The foundations of modernity were a reinforcing cycle of freedom, ideas, prosperity, and knowledge that created an ever-expanding capacity for further human action. Today, every person in a developed, democratic nation (plus a great many in other countries) have far more opportunities for human action than could be imagined 150 years ago. The capacity for human action increased even faster beginning in the middle of the twentieth century. In fact, many of the challenges we face today are the result of so much change happening so quickly that we outran our capacity to understand the consequences.

Currently, we have almost unlimited possibilities in many areas of life. As examples, we have numerous options for where we live, what type of work we do, the training we receive, health and medical care, plans for the future, the products and services we purchase, and how we spend leisure time. This expanding scope for human action came primarily from economic prosperity, which required enhanced productivity, which required increasing specialization, fragmentation, and complexity. Science and technology introduced ideas, processes, and devices many cannot fully understand. All of these things created a world that is more difficult to understand and navigate. Thus, the very system that increased our well-being and enlarged our scope for action also complicated our decision-making.

Increasing prosperity meant that more and more people could move up Maslow's motivational hierarchy. They could invest more time and resources in actions beyond what was required for basic living. However, as noted in the Principles section above, at the higher levels it becomes more difficult to decide what *ends* we should choose, and with a chosen *end*, it is more difficult to understand which *means* are most likely to be successful. Put differently, in the upper levels, it is easier for a person to choose *ends* that will not be satisfying when assessed in later years and to choose *means* that won't be recognized as unsuccessful until the distant future.

Today, we must overlay another challenge: increasing timeframes. At all levels of Maslow's pyramid, even the lower ones, our decisions must account for significantly longer times between an action and its result. For example, longer lifespans together with a phase of life called retirement requires that we take actions that will affect health and standard of living four or five decades in the future. Another example is voting on social issues that require action now but will produce assessable results many years in the future.

If an individual is considering their esteem, actualization, or transcendence twenty years in the future, there will be multiple ends which they imagine might satisfy their motivations, but there is no way to know with certainty. Furthermore, if a specific end is chosen, there will be multiple means which could be imagined to be effective, but again with much uncertainty. If they choose wealth, they may fail, or corrupt themselves or others, or succeed in gaining wealth but be unhappy. The same is true for fame or creating a legacy. Transcendence may be sought through ideologies, or maybe even through transhumanism. However, we've seen the tragedy of some ideologies, and the idea of something part human and part something else is largely unexplored.

The *ends* we include in our benefit scale, as well as the way in which we rank their priority, are influenced by multiple factors, some of which have changed a great deal in the past fifty years. The impact of intermediate institutions such as civic clubs and religious groups have declined. On a national average, the same is true for public education, the stability of families, and the impact of local communities. During the time that some influences were waning, others were increasing. Today, one of the most powerful shapers of thinking comes from advertising, mass communications, and social media. Stated generally, influences have moved from the focused and local to the broad and national.

If an award were given for what has had the greatest impact on human action (while at the same time remaining extremely subtle), it might go to our monetary system. Immediately following World War II a new monetary system was put in place for the free world. That system was replaced by another system in the early 1970s, one that governs all countries today. This system enabled an explosion of debt, which continues today. At one level, the effect of debt on human action is obvious. But the more powerful impact derives from the political, social, and economic structures that the monetary system enabled—all of which had a profound impact on human action.

How we understand the selection of *ends* and *means*, and the feedback of cause and effect, is critical. The influences briefly described above will be discussed throughout the book, with several chapters dedicated to specific aspects.

WORLDVIEW

"Our knowledge becomes constantly more specialized, more complicated, rather than more general. Something essential is lacking—namely a philosophical synthesis appropriate to the world we inhabit and see."
Peter Drucker

"A worldview is, as a theory, an interpretation of all things, and as a precept for action, an opinion concerning the best means for removing uneasiness as much as possible."
Ludwig von Mises

The Principles

Because it is an aspect of human nature, each person possesses an understanding of how the world works. *Worldview* is the name given to this comprehensive understanding. The content of a worldview can range from the big questions posed by religion and philosophy to the technical knowledge required by a person for economic production. The content will always include an understanding of how society functions. Stated broadly, a worldview is the collection of beliefs, knowledge, biases, skills, and experiences by which a person interprets their observations and experience and by which they make decisions that drive action.

Not everyone needs or wants a worldview with the same content. One difference depends on the role of the individual in a society. A subsistence farmer in the far reaches of a kingdom is likely to have a worldview much different in content than that of the king's worldview. Every person develops a worldview appropriate to their practical daily life. However, even among people in the same social context there is wide variation in the content of worldviews. For example, one person may primarily be interested in understanding only what is required for his immediate daily life while a neighbor may be interested in understanding things far removed from daily life, such as questions of meaning and philosophy. Likewise, one person may think that his community should pursue a common goal using one method while their neighbor is confident that only a completely different method will be effective. Differences in worldviews among people account for many of the benefits within a society as well as many of the conflicts.

Much of the content of a person's worldview comes to them automatically and depends on where and when they were born. Each person is born in a particular country that is part of a particular civilization. Their country has a history, culture, and language that implicitly shapes much of how they perceive and think and act. On top of that, every society intentionally passes along a worldview for the purpose of perpetuating the society. However, just because much of a person's worldview comes to them implicitly and through intentional effort does not prevent them from modifying their worldview as they come to understand the world through new experiences and knowledge.

Whether in a simple village or in today's complex world, the most important method by which a person adjusts their worldview is by observing the outcomes of actions taken by themselves and by others and then comparing those results against what the prevailing worldview says should have happened. Such analysis will either strengthen confidence in parts of the worldview or will motivate the person to question their understanding. The well-being and improvement of each person, and therefore of society, depends on this observe-analyze-adjust process (which in many fields of study is called a feedback loop).

Stated simply, we need a worldview because we have a built-in need to make sense of our world. If something happens to make our world unintelligible, if our worldview no longer reliably guides us in decisions and actions, we become stressed. If too many members within a society become stressed because their world no longer makes sense, the society will likely undergo major changes that may entail serious conflict.

Around the world and throughout history, the worldviews of societies address common categories of questions that arise out of human nature. However, the answers to specific questions within those categories vary a great deal depending on the time and place in history.

Present Characteristics

One way of describing this book is that it is about the development and understanding of worldviews of the modern citizen. Each chapter will look in detail at one or more worldview components that are particularly relevant to our present challenges and opportunities. What is required of this chapter is to briefly explore overarching themes that have shaped modern worldviews. Without such a big-picture sketch it is not possible to understand the significant transitions that took place and how those transitions formed our present circumstances. We must look at history to grasp this overview.

Population is a useful reference point against which to sketch the overview and has several advantages. It is the easiest and most accurate of social parameters to estimate or measure. It has meaning and significance for any society at any time. Finally, it is a useful proxy for economic production and for other activities that determine population growth.

For most of human history, population growth was extremely slow by modern standards. For example, for the first four hundred years of the current era (up to 400 CE), world population grew about 12%. For the next three 400-year periods, ending at 1600 CE, the growth was 16%, 64%, and 51% respectively. However, in the 400 years from 1600–2000 CE, an astonishing thing took place. World population growth increased more than 1000%, more than twenty times faster than the previous periods. Further, the standard of living for that huge population was also far better than in the year 1600. The essential question is, how was it possible, what happened, for the world to experience huge growth in both population and standard of living?

As is often true in history, the events and movements that capture our attention are often preceded by long periods of change and preparation. For several centuries preceding 1600, what we now know as Western Europe was rapidly gaining influence in the broader world. A few of the noteworthy developments within Western Europe during those centuries include the Renaissance, the Protestant Reformation, the Black Death, and the work of philosophers and scientists. Among the many important social changes was the rise of the merchant class, both in number and social esteem. By the middle of the 1600s, the mixture of ideas and changing circumstances reached a tipping point.

That tipping point increased the pace of work in philosophy and science. From philosophy came increasing justification for new perspectives on government, freedom, property, and economics. From science came a better understanding of the natural world, an explanation of things previously attributed to metaphysical causes, technology, and a general optimism that science could continuously improve the life of people. This time began what has been called the Age of Reason.

Christianity, represented primarily by the Catholic Church, had a huge influence in the development of Europe. However, beginning in the 1600s, the institutional Christian church experienced a long, slow decline in its influence. The reasons for this decline fall into two categories. First, there were internal problems, including corruption and conflict within Catholicism, conflicts between Catholicism and governments, and conflicts between the Catholic and Protestant churches. Second, in some cases, the philosophers and scientists were providing better answers and explanations to questions and problems than was the Church.

Although the historical record shows that many of the early philosophers and scientists had no intention of weakening the Church or Christianity, and in fact, often viewed their work as revealing the glory of God, it is nonetheless true that their work ultimately contributed to the declining influence of Christianity. This decline was facilitated by thinkers, few in number at first but growing over time, who explicitly argued that Reason would be a more effective guide to social development than would Christianity.

From the above points we can formulate two signal trends that have shaped our worldviews up to the present. Freedom, ideas, science and technology, and prosperity formed a reinforcing cycle in which each of those things steadily, if unevenly, progressed. This process was necessarily a cycle because everything we want to do requires resources. If material prosperity had not increased sufficiently to provide extra resources, progress in the other areas would have stopped, or at a minimum would have had little benefit for humankind. That is the first trend.

The second trend, which was also supported by the first trend, was a diminishing reliance upon authority and an increasing reliance upon reason and human action. The high respect and obedience given by the populace to the church and to the king slowly declined in favor of reason, science, and governance more closely aligned with the citizens.

Those two defining trends have been dominant influences for the past several centuries. However, in order to understand worldview development from 1950 onward, we must look at the exceptional events of the first half of the twentieth century. The three most significant events were World War I, the Great Depression, and World War II. Of the many effects and lessons stemming from those events, I will mention only a few which are most relevant in this book.

World War I was a strong refutation of the ideals on which Western Europe had built its civilization. The supremacy of Reason, the peace-protection of economic integration, the striving for justice and equality, and other high ideals derived from the Age of Enlightenment (Age of Reason) were shown to be inadequate by the ravages of the war. Amidst the intellectual confusion following World War I, conditions developed in Europe which led—only twenty years later—to the even more destructive Second World War.

The World Wars brought much more than a verdict against Enlightenment ideals. Europe, the preeminent world power for the previous 300 years, lay devastated. Science and technology, which had brought great benefit over the previous two centuries, proved equally applicable to weapons of destruction. Perhaps more troubling was the recognition that supposedly civilized and peace-loving people were capable of engaging in total war. Finally, the finishing act of World War II—the use of atomic weapons—demonstrated that the world would soon possess weapons capable of perhaps literally destroying most of the earth.

In addition to developments arising directly from war itself, two other derived effects had equal, if not greater, impact on worldviews. First, the size and scope of all governments increased tremendously as a result of the wars. Second, because of the economic devastation and the huge debt that resulted from the wars, a new type of monetary system was put in place.

Between the world wars, specifically the decade preceding World War II, much of the world experienced the Great Depression. What World War I did regarding Enlightenment ideals, the Great Depression did for assumptions underlying economic and monetary systems. How could prosperous times so quickly turn into poverty? How could so many people be employed one year and unemployed the next? Yet, it was not the economic deprivation as such that had the largest long-term impact on worldviews but rather what people came to believe about the answers to those questions.

Unlike Europe, which had begun doubting the free-market system decades earlier, this was not a major outcome of the Great Depression for the United States. What was of long-term significance for worldviews was a changing understanding of employment. The federal government was going to continually expand its role in providing full employment and in providing short-term financial protection when people became unemployed. That was the starting point. However, in subsequent decades, government policy related to employment and to "safety net" payments had significant economic and social impact.

These and other events of the first half of the twentieth century produced a reordered world compared to the close of the nineteenth century. In world affairs, the United States emerged as the dominant force economically and militarily. Many countries of the world lined up behind one of two competing ideologies: freedom and communism. Those countries that chose freedom moved steadily toward democracy as it is understood today. Those countries also began a long trend of increasing prosperity and health. Citizens of those countries saw less governmental and social restrictions on personal behavior. Finally, after World War II, the world has experienced no major wars. For free countries, this combination of relative peace, increasing freedoms, and increasing prosperity created social environments and personal opportunities never before seen in history.

Those new environments and opportunities resulted in an increasing rate of change in almost every domain of life. While at any point in time some people were concerned about particular changes or about the pace of change, the majority of people judged that the changes were beneficial and worth the cost. That statement is simply an axiom of democracy, for if the majority had decided that the changes were not worth the cost, people would have voted differently.

However, more than seventy years after the beginning of those trends, we are facing a number of problems that have so far proved intractable. A major claim of this book is that most of those problems are the result of unforeseen consequences of actions taken in earlier decades. Throughout this book we will explain those consequences and how they happened. We will look at why our worldview developed as it did and why we were unable to correct it sooner.

ECONOMICS

"There is, indeed, a most dangerous passage in the history of a democratic people. When the taste for physical gratifications amongst such a people has grown more rapidly than their education and their experience of free institutions, the time will come when . . . they lose sight of the close connection which exists between the private fortune of each of them and the prosperity of all."
Alexis de Tocqueville

"Man throughout history has been searching for the cure for poverty. . . That individual cure was Work and Saving. In terms of social organization, there evolved spontaneously from this, as a result of no one's conscious planning, a system of division of labor, freedom of exchange, and economic cooperation, the outlines of which hardly became apparent to our forebears until two centuries ago."
Henry Hazlitt

The Principles

I was initially reluctant to use *Economics* as the title for this chapter because today it conveys a meaning that obscures its essential nature. The word usually brings to mind professional economists employed by government and academia for the purpose of gathering data, producing national statistics, and creating mathematical models, all for the purpose of informing government policy. With that definition, the subject would not belong in a discussion of fundamental principles because such an understanding of economics is barely 100 years old, whereas we require an appreciation of economics that can apply from the times of early man until the present.

The word *economics* has its origin in a Greek word *oikos,* which was used when talking about the management of a household. The phrase "making a living" captures the idea. This simple understanding of economics will keep us grounded as we encounter the modern conception of economics as something that government does and which must be guided by complicated mathematical models. Working to improve our circumstances is a central and natural human action. We will see that the principles are simple, a fact hidden and confused by unnecessary government action.

All of economics is derived from two simple facts. First, humans need and want to consume; this is true from birth to death. A person *needs* food and shelter to survive. That is, they need to consume food for energy and materials for shelter. As circumstances improve such that they can operate higher up Maslow's pyramid, they *want* to consume goods and services for pleasure and esteem. People always seek to improve their circumstances, even if in small ways. Second, production must precede consumption. A person cannot consume what has not been produced. Food must be gathered, hunted, or farmed. Providing shelter requires material and labor. The first simple fact of economics comes from human nature, the second follows as a natural law.

Although the reality that production must come before consumption cannot be cheated for a society, it can be cheated by individuals or small groups. This happens because, as seen in the chapter on human nature, it is always true that a percentage of people within a society will violate the moral code. One group may decide that rather than contribute to production, they prefer to take what others have produced. Such taking requires violence or the threat of violence. Common methods used for this theft include robbery, raiding, and conquering. Historically, such activities have been easy to identify, and therefore a person or a society would use violence exercised via punishment or physical resistance to counter the theft.

Material prosperity is not the natural state of affairs. In fact, most people through most of history spent their time struggling to maintain a standard of living not much above survival. The means or modes of production were quite simple for thousands of years and changed extremely slowly. The productivity per person grew so little that it was essentially constant over a person's lifetime, and therefore the standard of living was constant. Of course, new knowledge and tools were developed over these thousands of years, but by today's standards, the number of innovations and their impact on productivity were small.

Because the production of food has necessarily been the primary focus of productive activity (economics) for most of human history and because the productivity gains were small, the population of the world grew slowly until the birth of modernity. It was simply not possible to provide food for more people. A corollary of this reality is that a large majority of people had to work to produce food. As a simplified example, if a family could only produce 5 percent more food than was required for their survival, then twenty families would have to be involved in food production for each family serving some other role in society. Thus, the growth of urbanization was limited as was the number of people who could be employed in ways that did not contribute to food production; for example, government, military, religion, and education.

Two mechanisms have always been part of economic activity no matter the simplicity or complexity of the underlying production system. One of these, exchange, was discussed earlier in the chapter on human action. It is almost always possible for individuals to improve their situation by exchanging goods and services with other people because people have different abilities and have access to different resources. Such exchanges may take place locally or, under the name of *trade*, may take place over great distances. The second mechanism came about in order to support exchange. Directly exchanging one good for another soon becomes cumbersome without using money as a medium of exchange. History reveals a fascinating array of objects that have been used as money by different societies. By and large, however, metals such as gold and silver became dominant beginning several thousand years ago.

Because of money's pivotal role in economic activity, it has always been a tool for those in power and for those who want power. How rulers use the monetary system for power may be the least appreciated reason for economic and social dysfunction. Money has, in fact, contributed to the decline of countries and empires.

Present Characteristics

We are obsessed with economic issues, which today must include not simply the age-old need to earn a living but also the complexity of today's economic system plus the effect of government on the economic structure. Economic activity has always been of primary importance for people because it is necessary for survival and for meeting many of our desires. But our situation today is fundamentally different, and this difference has much to do with our current challenges and problems. Today, governments attempt to manage economies, using GDP (gross domestic product) as the key measurement. Following World War II, and though not stated explicitly, both governments and citizens came to understand GDP as a proxy for quality of life. Citizens have in recent decades begun questioning this equivalence. Nonetheless, the social and political focus remains firmly directed at economic progress.

We will look at economics from multiple perspectives throughout the book. In this chapter, the task is to broadly characterize our economic environment.

Comparison to a simpler time may be helpful. Allow me to use a personal example to illustrate. As a young boy in the 1960s, I observed my grandfather's life as a farmer. In stereotypical fashion, he worked from sunup to sundown working on his economic enterprise. But I never once heard him talk about interest rates, globalization, the latest employment figures, the government deficit, or funding his retirement. Furthermore, his world was comprehensible. He knew where he fit, he knew on whom he depended and who depended on him. As I look back, I see no hint that he viewed his world as random or irrational. That doesn't mean he had control over his world. On the contrary, he had no control over the weather and only modest control over pests and other risks. In contrast, many employees today are one tiny part of a huge economic system that can seem incomprehensible and that can totally disrupt their lives in ways that are unpredictable and that may appear malevolent.

Much of our present social and political turmoil derives from economic issues. That is why it is essential that we as citizens have an appropriate understanding of how the various parts of our economic system function. Furthermore, economic forces lie behind many of our social issues. This integrated system is not simple or obvious in its workings. One of my goals for this book is to help explain how these systems work and what effects they have on society.

Our time is characterized by the production of goods and services. Growth in productivity and the resulting increase in population and standard of living not only increased following the devastation of the first half of the twentieth century, it accelerated. Today, we have an almost unbelievable selection of goods and services, most of which go well beyond what would be required for a modest standard of living. The consumption pattern of the past seventy years confirms that aspect of human nature in which people are always willing to engage in further consumption.

The desire to consume is so strong that as the monetary and financial system changed to make borrowing easier, many people were eager to go into debt in order to consume now and pay later. This willingness to postpone future payment for the enjoyment of present benefits resulted in increasing debt at every level of society, not only personal but also industry and government. As a result, formal debt plus unfunded liabilities are so high that together they represent another defining economic characteristic of our time.

Prosperity has now been the norm for several generations. As a result, more people assume it is natural and that our productive structure is on autopilot. This is a dangerous assumption because, as with all beneficial systems, our economic structure requires continuous attention and maintenance. Beneficial systems take a long time to build but can be broken quickly.

Governments have steadily grown in size and scope. Through monetary policy, fiscal policy, trade policy, and regulation, the federal government in particular has steadily grown in economic influence. Almost all economic decisions whether at the personal or organizational level must be made with an eye to what government has done and is likely to do. At present, the influence of government on economic affairs seems likely to continue growing. This large, if not yet dominant, government effect on economic activity may now be the most important economic characteristic.

Inflation is an important attribute of our economic system and is the result of intentional government action. (In this book, inflation means increase in prices, or the equivalent decrease in the purchasing power of money.) In the 100 years from 1920 to 2020, the purchasing power of one dollar dropped to seven cents. Compare that to the 100 years of the nineteenth century in which the purchasing power of one dollar increased to almost $1.50. As we shall see later, the inflation itself, as well as what caused the inflation, played an important role in creating many of today's problems.

Not only governments but also companies have grown in size. As with government, size brings power to these large private organizations. This concentration of power—in government and industry—is another distinguishing feature of our time. While recognizing that company revenue and a country's GDP can't strictly be compared, it nonetheless helps illustrate the point. If the revenue of the top 10 or 15 private companies were combined, the number would exceed the GDP of every country in the world excepting the five largest countries. These companies all have international operations. Thus, the CEO of a huge company commands more resources and may have more powerful international connections than do most heads of state.

Because it is true that very few things are free, what is the cost or downside of the free-market system that enabled the benefits discussed above? Reduced to a single word, a good answer would be *disruption.* Based upon several hundred years of experience with free market systems, we know this disruption can take many forms, including these: disrupting older, more stable systems; introducing the stress of competition; increasing the probability of unemployment; and creating social and economic inequality. Societies differ in their response to these disruptions, but in all cases each society must deal with ongoing tension between the benefits and downsides of free-market systems. Because disruption is inherent in our economic system, it is worth considering three categories of response within the last 150 years.

By the mid-1800s, a number of thinkers believed there must be a better way. The most important of these was Karl Marx. He freely admitted that the free-market system would steadily improve productivity and therefore produce more goods and services. However, he believed that the benefits were not worth the disruptive consequences. He believed free market economies would first move to socialism and then to communism, which would strike the ideal balance between prosperity, peace, and human dignity. His ideas were tested in massive experiments in the twentieth century. Many countries adopted socialism and communism. Before the century ended, it was clear that this first category of response to free markets had produced disastrous consequences. Tens of millions of people had died and hundreds of millions more had suffered deprivation, while in free-market countries benefits had been steadily multiplying.

The second category of response was from countries which wanted to retain the economic benefits of the free-market system while providing government programs to mitigate disruptions. This approach began in parts of Europe prior to 1900 and became the generally accepted policy for most of Europe by 1950. The United States began adopting this approach in the 1930s with unemployment insurance and has steadily increased the scope of mitigating policies. Under this approach, societies must strike a careful balance between minimizing disruptive effects while not damaging the productive power of free markets. Furthermore, these government policies are paid for by taking from one group of citizens and giving to another. Here also, society must find the right balance so that the transfer payments are seen as fair by all citizens.

The third category of response, which is recent and still developing, arose as more and more citizens were personally impacted by our growing social problems. People were not only impacted, they realized that solutions were not forthcoming. Leaders were not proposing believable solutions. A few examples of these problems are rising inequality, development of an underclass, unfunded liability, threats to freedoms, demographic pressures, concentrations of power, increasing transfer payments, and increasing debt. While the fundamental causes of these problems began decades ago, it was the "Great Recession" of 2008 that brought them into focus. The two most obvious manifestations of this third category of response are the political disruptions in the United States and Europe and the steadily worsening social and political divisiveness in the United States.

Finally, the last economic characteristic to be mentioned here is the world's monetary system. As we will see later, it is unlike any the world has witnessed previously. It has enabled many of our current problems, and its significance is equal to any other specific cause we might list. Yet, it is probably the least understood of all the driving forces. Over the last fifteen years, our understanding of the monetary system has become even more confused.

We will explore these characteristics in the coming chapters.

KNOWLEDGE, TOOLS, SCIENCE

"It is often difficult enough for the expert, and certainly in many instances impossible for the layman, to distinguish between legitimate and illegitimate claims advanced in the name of science."
F.A. Hayek

"Scientific truth is marvelous, but moral truth is divine and whoever breathes its air and walks by its light has found the lost paradise."
Horace Mann

The Principles

Science has, for several centuries, steadily grown as a shaping influence within society. As with the other fundamental subjects we are considering, we must grasp some underlying principles in order to understand the influence and role of science in our time.

The first principle to recognize is that knowledge, tools, and science (KTS) are as old as humanity, predating written history by tens of thousands of years. We know this, as one example, from archaeological records that show a steady, if extremely slow, evolution of stone tools that improved the capacity to obtain food, clothing, and shelter.

In previous chapters, we saw that human action is limited by the physical and intellectual environment. Stated differently, the expression of human action depends on available resources and the prevailing worldview. One specific example, as we saw in the worldview chapter, is the slow growth in productivity and population for thousands of years up to around 1600. That same pattern is seen in the development of KTS. A changing worldview opened up avenues for science, which in turn brought about changes in worldview, a cycle that has continued to this day.

Another principle is that the essential nature of KTS remains the same, whether we're talking about primitive tools from long ago or about the latest technology today. The process follows what was discussed in the chapter on human action: ideas, resources, experiments, assessments, adjustments. Consider a simple illustration of the development of a stone harpoon, which took place approximately 80,000 years ago. First, a person had to come up with the idea that such a tool would be useful. Then they had to invest time to find a stone that could be shaped. The shaping itself would take time because it would have to be done with yet another type of stone. After some initial work, a version of the tool could be tried. Based upon how well it worked, modifications would be made in the next version. Eventually, the best rock and the best shape and the best means of attachment would have been developed. At every stage of the process, the person had to invest time and energy. We know from the archaeological record that such tools were successfully made and that they enabled people to more easily catch larger fish, an advancement that benefited the entire community.

A corollary principle is also illustrated in the above example. KTS and material well-being are integrally linked.

On occasion, the accumulation of KTS reaches a level that causes significant changes in the worldview of the society, which in turn may result in new social and rulership structures, new means of economic production, or new views of what is possible. By way of examples consider the emergence of agriculture, the Bronze and Iron Ages, ocean navigation, the ability to manage empires, gun powder, the European Renaissance, the Enlightenment, and information technology. While it is not possible to predict what these accumulations will be nor their timing, it is a principle that they will occur.

The final principle to highlight is that the acquisition of knowledge and the development of tools require resources. At a minimum, an individual must have the time and the appropriate setting and sufficient energy to make observations and come up with potentially useful ideas. In most cases, however, ideas alone are not enough to benefit society. The ideas must be turned into processes or tools, which will require additional resources. For example, in the harpoon illustration above we could speculate that other members of the community agreed to invest more of their time and effort to provide food for the individual who was learning to make the harpoons so that the new tool could be made available sooner. Stated generally, the acquisition of knowledge and the development of useful tools and processes are limited by resources.

Present Characteristics

As we saw concerning economics in our world today, the importance of KTS is not that it is a fundamentally new human activity but that it has become much more central to our lives. The reinforcing cycle among worldview, economics, and KTS, which began its acceleration in the 1600s, is largely responsible for what we experience today. For this book, specific examples of KTS are not what is important. We don't need to look at particular scientific breakthroughs or the still-expanding world of information or bioengineering. What we need to understand is the role KTS played in the development of our current worldview and how it contributed to some of our major problems.

Up to this point in the chapter, I've used KTS (knowledge, tools, science) in order to emphasize that these aspects of thinking and action have always been part of human history. Now, when speaking specifically of the present, I will sometimes use *information* in place of *knowledge* because we often speak of the information age and of the volume of information produced. Likewise, *technology* will often be used in place of *tools*.

Science will still be used, but the term needs an expanded definition. In discussing principles above, I used *science* to refer to the rudiments of the scientific method that have always been an aspect of human activity. However, soon after the advent of writing and the development of civilizations, science started to become more formal and more systematic. Furthermore, the scientific method was applied to subjects beyond the immediate making of tools. Today, *science* is used in several ways. It may still refer simply to the means and methods of science. It may also represent science analogous to how we speak of government, economics, and finance. That is, *science* might refer to the activities, the results, the institutions, and the systemic influences of anything labeled as science. Finally, *science* is sometimes used to mean not only the fundamental work of scientists but also the resulting technology. Therefore, while science as a human activity is not new, science as understood today does represent a new social influence, just as economics as understood today is a new concept in history. Unless a distinction is necessary, in the remainder of the book, I will use *science* in its broadest meaning, which includes information, technology, direct science work, and its role as a social force.

With the twin engines of economics and science linked together, the rapid growth in material well-being and population has continued for several hundred years. However, by the early 1800s, those engines did not always share the same approval and stature with the public or with rulership. Economic models and structures caused disruption and discontent, as we saw earlier. In some cases, of course, specific technology was also disruptive and was met with social resistance. But for the most part, the contributions of science to health, knowledge, and productivity were held in esteem. This esteem, it turns out, was to play an important role in the early twentieth century. But to appreciate what happened, we need a brief digression to broadly characterize the fields of science.

Prior to 1900, most progress in science came from *hard* fields such as mathematics, engineering, physics, chemistry, and biology. In this context *hard* does not refer to difficulty of understanding but to objectivity. "Objective" means that there is a provably correct answer with which everyone would agree. Hard domains can be investigated by repeated experiments by different scientists in order to confirm theories and technology. In most cases, the results from hard sciences follow shortly after the experiment is complete. That is, scientists usually don't have to wait for years or decades to see the results of their experiments. In *hard* domains, it is almost always possible to conclusively demonstrate that certain actions cause predictable and quantifiable results.

Soft subjects, on the other hand, are those in which there is no provably correct answer or that the answer cannot be known for a long time. Fields such as sociology, psychology, and economics are *soft*. Most of the soft sciences we recognize today did not exist 150 years ago, or if they did, they had an insignificant role in society. An important distinction between hard and soft is that in soft domains the experts often don't agree on how experiments should be tried or even which ones should be tried, and they often disagree on which results are good or bad, and correct or incorrect. Soft domains are characterized by having multiple, uncontrollable potential causes influencing something "non-mechanistic" such as a person. In these *soft* cases, the cause-effect connection will be ambiguous, with multiple possibilities argued convincingly by different people.

In a later chapter about power, we will see that citizens must believe that government power is legitimate. Science helps support the legitimacy of modern government in two ways. First, and most obviously, government directs and funds science to support the material well-being of citizens, and it is this material well-being, which includes increasing prosperity, that is the most fundamental pillar for government legitimacy. The hard sciences have produced most of those results that are visible and much-discussed in public forums. The second way in which science plays a role in the legitimacy of government power is more implicit and far less obvious because it involves soft sciences. This second way receives less public attention even though its social impact is as large as that of the hard sciences. In recent years, this soft science basis of government has arguably become more important than the results of hard science. Therefore, we will study it in more detail and will do so by looking at the most important of the soft sciences: economics.

For the most part, the field of economics prior to 1900 was not regarded as a science comparable to physics, chemistry, and others. However, as economies became more complicated and as government became more involved in and responsible for economic activity, some people looked at the success of the hard sciences and decided that economics should adopt the methodology and aspire to the predictive certainty of the hard sciences. They thought a science of economics could be as productive in explaining, predicting, and controlling economic activity as the hard sciences had been in the physical and natural domains. This fit with the general mood of the time in which science seemed capable of almost anything. Therefore, beginning around 1900, work in economics became increasingly mathematical and theoretical. This was a necessary step for economics to assume a major role in making government policy appear legitimate, something we will examine in later chapters.

From this point forward in the book, I will drop the use of the descriptors *hard* and *soft* as they apply to science unless the distinction is important for the subject at hand. In common usage, *science* usually refers to the hard sciences if the distinction is important at all. There are a couple of reasons for that usage. Most of the benefits, power, and easily seen risks associated with science come from the hard domains. On the other side, people hold mixed views of soft fields and often disagree about their findings and indeed their importance.

As already noted, science provided power and benefits long before the twentieth century, but it was in that century that science went to a new level. If we were to select an iconic beginning for this new level, it might be the development of atomic weapons in the 1940s. Suddenly, the world understood that it now possessed the ability to destroy itself. From that point forward, the benefits of science increasingly also brought risks. Nuclear energy is a good example: the same science that produced weapons could also be used to produce abundant electricity. Today, we are well aware of this plus-minus characteristic of science, including examples such as the food industry, pesticides, pharmaceuticals, information technology, and biomedical research as a small subset. Often, the negative side of a contribution from science is not intentional; it is a natural side effect, and it may not be discovered until many years after the introduction of the technology. This characteristic of today's science places a responsibility on citizens to make difficult assessments.

A common subject today is the stress that comes from the rapid pace of change in society. Science is one of the chief engines of change. Increasing prosperity enabled huge increases in the various fields of science. The rapid rate of change has made it difficult for the average citizen as well as for government agencies to keep up with the necessary assessments of negative consequences. These consequences include not only the direct effects of using science but also, increasingly, the creation of difficult moral issues.

Because science has become so specialized and because some of the consequences of science-related decisions don't show up until many years later, society faces a challenge in monitoring and controlling science. Society's decision-makers often lack the knowledge and experience required to understand the fundamentals of science and the technology derived from it. As a result, decision-makers may fail to grasp the short-term implications of a decision, and they may not even know how to think about the potential longer-term impacts. In recent decades, the dilemma has become more urgent because new developments in science and technology can have large-scale effects within society. In such cases, the decision-making is political as much as technical. That is, the decisions cannot be left totally to scientific experts who are not directly accountable to citizens through the voting booth. These cases are not just difficult from a technical point of view; they also create real tensions in a democracy, such as those arising from questions of freedom and property rights.

As if those were not challenges enough, we now face the biggest challenge of all regarding how science is to be developed, used, and regulated. For several centuries, science enjoyed a good reputation for the honesty, integrity, and good intentions of the individuals involved. However, over recent decades, science has steadily lost credibility because some scientists have compromised principles and integrity in the pursuit of government money or under the influence of government power or to conform to the social opinion of one group or another.

The credibility problem for science extends beyond simple politicizing results and communications. People who work in the fields of science, like those in many other areas, have been caught up in the ubiquitous pressure for quick results. For companies, the focus is profit and public perception. For nonprofit organizations such as universities, government agencies, think tanks, and others, the focus is building a reputation and obtaining funding from government and donors. In addition to competition among institutions, people within the institutions compete with each other for promotions and stature.

This pressure causes two behaviors that damage the credibility of science. First, the rush to produce research results, technical papers, and position papers encourages people to publish their work without sufficient verification. Second, because of the political and government influence on assessments and funding, people working in science have an incentive to produce results that meet the current social and political views. These behaviors bring damaging consequences. Increasingly, "experts" contradict each other; papers and results are retracted due to mistakes; papers and results are found to be intentionally biased—in some cases fraudulent—to support social or political opinion; advice from government agencies and other institutions is later proven not only wrong but harmful. A good example includes anything related to climate change and control.

Anyone who wants to spend a little time can easily observe the behaviors and consequences just noted. However, science is experiencing a more serious change. In the chapter on worldview, we noted that science earned its credibility over a long period of time because it could explain things and produce results where previous sources of authority, namely the structures of rulership and religion, could not. As a result, science became an increasingly trusted authority. During this long shift, a government might appeal to science in the same way that a government a few centuries ago might have appealed to religion.

Eventually, following a long process, science began to morph into a belief system. As we saw in the chapter on human nature, the need for a belief system is built into us. We will explore this in more detail in an upcoming chapter on belief systems. A name was given to this extension of science into a belief system: scientism. Unfortunately, it is part of human nature to go too far in promoting, defending, and coercing others in support of a deeply held belief system. A supposedly objective field like science is not immune from this aspect of human nature.

For those to whom science has become scientism, the motivations to depart from the historical integrity of science go beyond personal gain. Rather than open inquiry, debate, and a search for a better description of reality, we increasingly see the opposites. What is true or what represents reality is sometimes decided by social or political forces. Selected bits of evidence are taken as absolutely conclusive, ignoring contrary evidence. The prevailing belief then becomes doctrine that serves a role analogous to the doctrines of traditional religion. Two areas that illustrate this behavior today are (1) anything related to the climate, and (2) handling of pandemics.

History shows that adherents to a belief system will often feel justified, even obligated, to suppress heretics—defined as anyone who disagrees with the prevailing doctrine. Sometimes, zealots go further, not only suppressing or persecuting those who think differently but coercing them to convert to the "correct" doctrine. While in times past this coercion may have involved conquest, torture, or death, today the coercion involves financial, social, and reputational loss.

Those who practice scientism—as is true with many belief systems—may believe they are helping society by suppressing heretics. Today we see scientists losing their jobs, having their work attacked on prejudicial rather than objective terms, and losing funding for their research or projects. Citizens who are not scientists are also castigated and punished for questioning the chosen doctrine.

Conditions for the rise of scientism have been developing for decades. However, since the early years of this century, the practice of scientism has accelerated dramatically in scope and intensity. A reporter could easily find examples other than those just mentioned.

Scientism presents two risks for society. One risk is the objective damage resulting from scientific work that is intentionally corrupted or presented in a misleading manner. However, that risk has a counterforce: reality. That is, eventually reality will prove itself. The more serious risk is that the valuable role science has played in society will become corrupted. Citizens will increasingly take a negative view of science and of what they hear from scientists and from others who make claims in the name of science. Because of this distrust, it will become increasingly difficult to implement beneficial policies for the protection, health, and general well-being of society.

Now, let us imagine that scientism disappears and science returns to serving society in the best possible manner. Even then, we would still need to accept that science is limited. Science cannot provide the wisdom to manage science or any other domain which broadly impacts society. How to obtain such wisdom is one of society's biggest challenges.

POWER AND FREEDOM

"The truth is that the State in which the rulers are most reluctant to govern is always the best and most quietly governed, and the State in which they are most eager, the worst."
Plato, *The Republic*

"Freedom is never more than one generation away from extinction. We didn't pass it to our children in the bloodstream. It must be fought for, protected, and handed on for them to do the same."
Ronald Reagan

The Principles

Power is the primary driver of history. Power is a far more commanding force and value than freedom. Evidence of the exercise of power is clear throughout history, whereas freedom as it is understood today can rarely be identified as shaping history until the modern period. Stated in terms of human action, the desire for power has a much greater impact upon societies than does the desire for freedom. Furthermore, power and freedom are always in tension with each other. Without some knowledge of power, it is impossible to understand the workings within a society and the interaction among societies.

Power structures have existed in all societies because such structures are necessary. From the chapter on human nature, we know the following things are relevant to the development of power structures: 1) a tiny percentage of people will possess an extremely high desire for power, 2) almost every person in a society is highly motivated to obtain security and physical well-being, 3) there appears to be an innate desire for hierarchy. In addition, experience teaches that security and productivity are improved with organized activity, and organization requires hierarchy of a form that entails power. Finally, a power structure may be imposed from outside a society through conquest by a foreign society. Power is gained and used because it is desired and because it is effective in achieving goals.

Five thousand years of history reveal three common power structures: rulership (government), economic (production), and creed (religion, belief systems). These three domains look different and interact differently depending on the specifics of a society. In some cases, the three merge to operate essentially like one structure. More commonly, there is a mixture of competition and cooperation among them. As a general rule, those in the rulership structure will make use of the economic and religious structures in their pursuit of power. The natural corollary to that rule is that the economic and religious structures will appeal to rulership for help within their domains. Much of the drama of history comes from the interplay of these three structures with each other, with the citizenry, and with other societies. This interplay may be honorable and peaceful; it may also be violent, oppressive, and subversive.

For those who desire power and then obtain it, their tendency is to find ways to increase power. In the rulership domain (government), they are limited by two things: resources and what the citizenry will tolerate. Government relies on the economic production of citizens to fund rulership operations. For most of history, economic productivity was not high enough to support large governments like we have today. However, in all cases, if government tries to take too much of society's production, the people will respond by reducing their production or, in extreme cases, by rebelling. The ultimate limit comes when the citizens believe that it is worth fighting to the death to resist power. A ruling power with no citizens will cease to exist.

Citizens will support, or maybe simply tolerate, a rulership structure only if they see it as legitimate. What defines legitimate for a society depends upon its circumstances and worldview. People in the rulership structure not only have power, they enjoy privileges and wealth far above the average citizen. As long as a large majority of citizens assess the situation to be reasonable within their worldview, the society will be stable. If that assessment changes such that citizens believe the arrangement is unjust, the society will become unstable. While the issue of legitimacy is most often relevant to the rulership structure, it sometimes applies to the economic structure also.

Every society operates by a set of *shoulds* and *should nots*. In a small, simple society, these rules may be unwritten and consist of commonly known and accepted norms. But in larger, more complex societies, the rulership will create formal, written laws to inform citizens what is required. Such law codes have been discovered dating to 4,000 years ago. Society works best when formal laws derive from existing cultural or common rules. That is, ideally, formal laws are consistent with and support the prevailing worldview of society, from which all informal rules have developed.

Before proceeding, I need to tighten the language above by making use of terms common today. I used *cultural*, *common*, and *worldview* in reference to informal rules. Today, the term *natural law* is often used to encapsulate these informal rules. (Here, *natural law* is used in the legal sense, not that of moral codes.) *Natural law* carries the meaning of what is considered right, fair, and just by ordinary citizens, values that have traditionally and commonly been the practice of citizens in daily life. What I called the formal law is known as *positive law* (from *to posit*, as opposed to what is negative).

At times, those in power may want to impose positive laws not in keeping with natural law. If the resulting gaps between the positive and the natural law are few and impact the lives of citizens in relatively minor ways, society can still function well. However, if the gaps continue to grow, it will harm society. Citizens may lose respect for positive law in general or may outright disobey the positive laws that conflict with natural law. In general, rulership can only enforce large gaps between positive and natural law by the exercise of force, and the larger the gap, the larger the force required. How these principles of positive and natural law and obedience or force play out depends on the particular circumstances of the society.

Freedom is not a single, well-defined concept. For example, a society may have restricted or wide freedom when it comes to foreign rule, selection of rulers, speech, religion, employment, property, and personal freedom. It is possible, for instance, to imagine a monarchy that provided most of those freedoms with the exception of selecting the king. What is meant by freedom in one society might be considered a burden in another society. Another way in which freedoms have been restricted, one that continues today in many places, is that some groups within a society have freedoms others do not.

Freedom is not natural, not in the sense that it automatically happens; nor is it common. Freedoms are rare, hard to achieve, and easily lost. That is true not only because freedom must be won from power but because each increase in freedom requires more personal responsibility from citizens. History offers multiple examples of citizens giving up freedom, or the opportunity for freedom, in exchange for the promise of security or prosperity—most often resulting in citizens having less of each rather than more.

Any exercise of power, especially rulership power, must always result in reduced freedom for some person or group. This is necessarily true because otherwise the use of power would not have been required. Sometimes, the exercise of power is driven by one group of citizens petitioning the rulership to act against another group of citizens. What matters for the quality of life in a society is the wisdom and knowledge that guides the exercise of power. Leadership matters.

I want to highlight three key lessons from history that are of special relevance to this book. First, power structures develop naturally and tend to increase while freedoms require effort to obtain and tend to decrease without constant maintenance of the necessary conditions. Second, when there is disagreement that can't be settled by other means, those in power will resort to coercion or violence. Whatever freedoms existed in the society are likely to be diminished or destroyed.

Third, we have considered principles related to power and freedom that have proved valid over time no matter what particular forms of power structures prevailed within a particular society. That does not mean particular societies at various times in history have not thought they had set up an arrangement that was better than all other systems that preceded it. There seems to be something in human nature that thinks, "This time is different; the old principles no longer apply." However, as I said at the beginning of this book, and as all historical experience confirms, the principles are timelessly valid.

Present Characteristics

One easily overlooked characteristic of our time is the newness of our power structures. In other chapters, we look specifically at the spheres of economics and belief systems. Therefore, here we will primarily focus on power and freedom related to rulership.

The newness of the dominant rulership structures needs to be emphasized. It is tempting to think modern democracy is over 200 years old, and at some level, that is true. However, strictly speaking, democracy as it is understood today is more recent due both to its formal structure and to the circumstances in which it functions. For example, the United States did not effectively have full suffrage until the middle of the twentieth century. Much of Western Europe did not become modern democracies until well into the twentieth century. Japan began the process of transitioning to democratic forms of rule following World War II. By 1960, many countries had democracies operating similar to today's democracies, and that group of countries produced a large majority of the world's GDP. This was a new world configuration.

Before we can productively describe our circumstances today, we require some definitions and context. The words *democracy* and *freedom* are often used interchangeably because the countries that provide the greatest number and degree of freedoms are democracies. However, to understand power and freedom we require a more careful definition of those words.

Democracy is frequently used to mean a set of benefits, specifically personal freedom and prosperity, which, it is assumed, can be obtained by letting people vote for their rulers and by making markets more free. Multiple experiences from the past 70 years show that these are necessary but not sufficient requirements. Examples include the fall of the Soviet Union, the Arab Spring, and ongoing, repeated attempts by numerous Latin American countries including Argentina, Bolivia, Peru, and Venezuela. It takes much more than a formal electoral system and some movement toward a market economy.

In general, a society must grow and develop the necessary understanding, habits, mindset, institutions, and other prerequisites necessary for a free and prosperous society. Furthermore, once those necessary aspects exist and are functioning well in a society, they must be maintained. Otherwise, freedom and prosperity will take the natural path of decay, resulting in decreasing freedom and prosperity. This is an important consideration for the United States today.

Rarely will a people desire freedom for its own sake and as its own reward. Rather, in most cases, people desire freedom—usually equated with democracy—as a path to a better life, which in modernity has largely come to mean improved material well-being. When a country decides to change from their existing system of governance and establish "democracy," it is likely to fail for the reasons noted above. That country will then decide that "democracy" does not work, in which case it most likely returns to a system similar to what existed prior to attempting "freedom." In some cases, with Latin America providing good examples, a country may ostensibly work toward democracy for decades before giving up and returning to an old system.

I've spent time talking about these failures not because the specifics for any one situation are important for this book but rather to emphasize what is of crucial importance. A democracy that provides freedom and the opportunity for prosperity, two core American ideals, requires a great deal of time and effort to create, followed by ongoing maintenance and defense. Democracy, in this sense, is more than voting and more than economic freedom. It is a way of life, a way of ordering all aspects of a society.

The founders of American democracy understood the principles discussed earlier. They also understood the risks of democracy. Nonetheless, they decided that a democratic republic form of government offered the best opportunity for human flourishing. They designed the Constitution and Bill of Rights to mitigate the natural problems that arise from power and from democracy. Even so, they explicitly acknowledged that the system of governance they created was not sufficient on its own. The freedoms granted under this new mode of government could only survive if citizens continue to process the necessary virtue, shared beliefs, commitment to democratic principles, and personal responsibility required of citizen rulers.

The founders were particularly mindful of two threats to such a democracy. One of the threats was the development of competing factions. The second was the unequal distribution of resources that naturally arise in a free society. The first threat was addressed by the structural details of the Constitution, though that alone would not be sufficient. Both threats require a virtuous people with a shared desire for the well-being of all citizens, something that has to be worked out among citizens. In short, the founders were aware that the United States was embarking on an historic experiment in rulership.

With that background, we are prepared to describe our current situation. As stated in the Introduction, I'm writing this book in response to serious challenges we face as a society. We certainly have problems connected to power and freedom, but we also have many strengths. The United States has more than 200 years of experience in living as a democratic society; we are practiced in the art of democracy. We have many institutions that provide structure and protection both for freedoms and for power. The majority of citizens still carry a desire for freedom and responsibility and flourishing. Finally, and most importantly, it remains possible for citizens to bring about change because the power structures can neither keep us from voting nor force us to vote as directed. Citizens have the freedom to vote in the political, social, and economic spheres. This capacity of citizens to change society is a cornerstone of this book.

The most common and also the least useful descriptions of social phenomena are those that describe symptoms. For example, we commonly encounter terms like divisiveness, polarization, and gridlock. Or a specific problem may be elevated as representing many problems; today, that representative problem would probably be inequality in its various forms. However, lamenting over those surface symptoms and attempting to solve the problems by masking the symptoms will not resolve anything. In fact, attempting to solve a particular problem in isolation is more likely to create further problems than fix anything. Rather, we require proper understanding of fundamental forces within society. This book is my contribution to that effort.

Each of the following characterizations of power and freedom in the United States will be discussed in more detail throughout the book. Therefore, here we need only a brief overview to establish the larger picture.

Whatever is good or bad in our present circumstances is the product of decisions made over many decades. Earlier, we sketched the events of the first half of the twentieth century as well as the new world order that resulted. Here, we pick up the story in 1945, at the close of World War II. Americans were eager to forget the destructive and stressful first half of the century and resume building prosperous and happy lives. Government was huge and powerful compared to only fifty years earlier. To a large extent, citizens assessed that the government had done an adequate job, perhaps even a good job, of navigating the previous forty years. Furthermore, this was a time of optimism about the possibility of combining science, management, and economics to govern a nation "scientifically." Thus, after 1945, an implicit bargain began forming between the citizenry and those in rulership positions (people sometimes referred to today as "ruling elites").

This bargain morphed into an implicit social contract that could be summarized as follows. Citizens handed over the management of the country to elected officials and to a rapidly growing administrative arm of government consisting of experts in fields such as economics, science, and defense. In exchange, the ruling class was to provide a safe environment that allowed citizens to exercise economic and social freedoms in pursuit of a flourishing life. The essence of the bargain was that citizens expected ever-expanding economic gains and personal fulfillment.

For about five decades, this bargain appeared to be working well. Material well-being steadily increased. Each generation came to expect that the following generation would be better off. Along the way, some astute observers could see that long-term problems were developing and were not being addressed. Nevertheless, expectations of an ever-improving world became normalized.

As the twenty-first century approached, however, a growing number of citizens began questioning the arrangement. Problems, both actual and potential, were becoming more obvious. The situation was ripe for a catalyst or tipping point. Such a point arrived with the financial crisis of 2008. The details of that crisis and its implications are discussed in other places in this book. Here, the important point is that a wider range of citizens began seriously questioning long-standing economic and social arrangements. In doing so, they were questioning the assumptions of the implicit bargain struck almost 60 years previous. The bargain came clearly into view with the tumultuous presidential election of 2016 which manifested a strong reaction against the "ruling elites" and put Donald Trump in the White House.

The United States did not suddenly become a polarized, divisive, gridlocked country. Rather, those attitudes and behaviors had been forming for years and were driven by economic and social forces going back even further (many of those forces will be discussed later). What occurred, as is often the case, is that specific events brought into the open and accelerated what had already been happening.

The financial crisis of 2008 was the crucial event that allowed us to recognize and identify what was taking place economically and socially, while the election of 2016 was the crucial event that generated political and social responses to those trends.

Following the 2016 election, the divisiveness and polarization not only accelerated, they resulted in intense acrimony not only toward and among elected officials and the ruling elite but also among ordinary citizens.

We are now ready to consider our present circumstances as just described and look at how they impact the exercise of power and freedom.

First, and at a broad level, we observe more people doubting the legitimacy of the rulership structure. Although perhaps few citizens think explicitly in terms of the implied bargain or social contract mentioned earlier, it is, in fact, that implicit bargain that is being called into question. Stated simply, citizens have progressively yielded power to the rulership structure and are now seeing that the expected benefits are decreasing. For most citizens who are assessing legitimacy, the issues have to do with policies and outcomes, with benefits received in exchange for power yielded. However, a small group of citizens now believe that the founding principles and founding documents of the United States are themselves not legitimate. In this view, both the history and the governing principles of the United States need to be rewritten. I mention this second group of citizens only to highlight the extent to which legitimacy is being questioned. It is an extreme view and one which will not be considered further in this book.

This questioning of legitimacy represents, in my opinion, the beginning of a growing reappraisal of the implicit bargain that formed in the middle part of the last century in which citizens yielded power to a rulership class in hope that those rulers would manage society for the flourishing of all citizens. Already, in response to the 2016 and 2020 elections, some leaders in government, business, and other key institutions are scrambling to figure out how to respond. So far, the responses are simply reactions. Some of these reactions have negative implications for both power and freedom in the United States.

In a free country such as the United States, citizens have three broad avenues by which they can influence the opinion and behavior of other citizens: persuasion, the market, and government. For this chapter, market influence is less important and will be set aside. For multiple reasons, the federal government has become the preferred avenue of influence. First, the level of divisiveness and acrimony have made persuasion very difficult, a reality we can hope is only temporary. Second, the federal government is now hugely more powerful than state and local governments. Its scope now reaches almost every facet of society. The administrative agencies of the federal government and the federal courts together with the executive and legislative branch wield unprecedented power. Third, a noticeable shift has occurred among many citizens who are now willing to use coercion rather than persuasion to influence other citizens. That is, a growing number of citizens are willing to infringe upon freedoms in order to advance particular policies. Fourth, because persuasion seems impossible, because some citizens are willing to coerce other citizens, and because the federal government has almost unlimited power, people realize that the most efficient and sure means of influence is to get control of the federal government.

The presidential election of 2020 gave a preview of what happens under the circumstances described above. When enough citizens begin questioning the legitimacy of the power structures—the rulership structure in particular—and when enough citizens feel threatened by coercion, society becomes less stable. In that election, some on each side were convinced the country was in danger of collapse if the other side won. Following the election, charges of fraud produced acrimonious debate which furthered division. Finally, we saw violence in the capitol on inauguration day. Such episodes make it easier to see the possibility of "tyranny under democracy." As we saw in the discussion of principles above, any form of government will move toward an abuse of power unless it can be constrained. In a democracy, the restraint must come from citizens committed to democratic principles.

A description of power and freedom is not complete unless we also look at what is taking place beyond the formal domain of politics. Human nature operating under freedom has a tendency to confuse freedom with license. That fact was recognized in the earliest experiments of democracy 2,500 years ago. Sustainable freedom requires a careful balance between rights and responsibilities. Freedom turns into license when citizens want to be free of all constraints on their actions, including the restraints of natural consequences.

Throughout this book, we will look at the exercise of power and freedom from multiple perspectives for the purpose of grasping what citizens must understand and do in order to solve the problems we have now and the ones we are facing. This will entail careful analyses of the underlying reasons that brought us to this point.

BELIEF SYSTEMS

"It is commonly said and known that each civilization has its own religion."
Huston Smith

"In politics, as in religion, it is equally absurd to aim at making proselytes by fire and sword."
Alexander Hamilton

The Principles

Belief systems have always been a powerful force in any group, whether as small as a tribe or as large as a civilization. This remains true today. Belief systems are powerful because they are a fundamental part of human nature. Every person has a belief system. It may be based on a philosophy of life, an ideology, or on what have traditionally been called religions. Belief systems are built into the worldview of a society. In some cases, the belief system of a society may be the dominant influence on many aspects of the worldview. As we saw earlier, the prevailing worldview of a society determines the characteristics of the rulership and economic power structures.

As a point of clarification, I am using *belief system* rather than the more traditional *religion* in this discussion, even when talking of historical systems. The reason will be clear below when we look at characteristics of our time in which *religion* carries connotations that confuse our thinking.

Belief systems can be quite different in some ways. For example, some belief systems will have a formal institutional structure while others will have almost none. The Catholic Church and Confucianism are respective examples. Those two belief systems also illustrate a difference with regard to God, the gods, or the supernatural. God is absolutely central to the Catholic Church while the supernatural plays a minor role in Confucianism. Other differences and other examples could be discussed, but they are not central to this book.

However, all belief systems share common characteristics important for the purposes of this book. All belief systems have something to say about what is true or not, how things ought to be or how they ought to work, and how people should and should not behave. These beliefs are intended for the good of those who subscribe to the belief system. It is largely through these beliefs and rules that a belief system shapes the worldview of a society. This is of great importance because, as we saw earlier, the worldview of a society largely determines the nature of the society and the extent to which its people flourish.

Another characteristic important for our purposes is that the power inherent in belief systems must always interact with the rulership structure. Those who wish to exercise rulership power must always decide how to deal with the power of belief systems. The two examples from above are again useful. For 2,000 years, the institutional Christian church has at times cooperated and at other times fought with those in rulership. At various times, the church tried to depose rulers, and rulers tried to destroy the church. Although Confucianism did not have an institutional structure, rulers at times supported those who taught the ways of Confucius, and at other times persecuted the teachers. The tension between rulership and belief systems continues today, alternating between cooperation, competition, and attempted destruction.

In addition to the potential conflict between belief systems and the rulership structure, belief systems are also a common source of conflict among groups within a society or between different societies. This potential for conflict is fueled by two sources. It is human nature to want others to agree with us, to see things the way we see them. For issues of minor importance, the desire to have other people agree with us is likely to be very weak. But when issues touch upon what is right and wrong, what should or should not be, how things ought to be, which god is supreme, and other elements of belief systems, the need for agreement can be quite strong. History offers countless examples of violence generated by differences in belief systems.

The second source of conflict is more direct. Some belief systems call for adherents to convert other people to adopt the belief system. In most cases, those who hold to a particular belief system may simply be called to attempt to peacefully convince others that they should adopt the preferred belief system. Some belief systems, however, advocate the use of violence, if necessary, to convince others. As it turns out, however, the dividing line between peaceful persuasion and violence is not clear.

As we noted in the chapter on human nature, many personal characteristics follow a distribution curve in which most people are near the average but in which a very small percentage of people exhibit extreme behaviors and capacities. This distribution applies to how people respond to or live out their belief system. Therefore, even within a peaceful belief system, there will be some individuals who are so convinced of its truth and value that they judge it is appropriate to use pressure, coercion, or violence to further the adoption of their belief system. Such people are sometimes called fundamentalists or zealots, and every belief system is susceptible to this phenomenon. Likewise, within a belief system that calls for coercion or violence in the conversion of others, there will be some believers who personally choose to avoid the use of coercion or violence.

To provide concrete examples of what was just discussed, consider Christianity and Islam. Christian teaching calls for peaceful persuasion, yet history offers examples in which zealots believed force was appropriate. Islam teaches that coercion and violence are justified for conversion of others, yet many Muslims do not personally use forceful means. Other belief systems could be used as examples; I chose these because they are well-known.

A society, indeed entire civilizations, depend on a belief system (it may be called a religion or a creed). Rulers have recognized this for millennia. If there was not a single belief system, then there was either a dominant one or there were multiple compatible ones. This is a necessity because of the nature of belief systems. They specify or guide so many things in a society that coherence is not possible if the differences are many.

Belief systems largely determine values. When cherished values are threatened, conflict will always follow.

Present Characteristics

Many people would say that the most obvious characteristic of our time regarding belief systems is that religion is becoming less important. In fact, I suggest that the defining characteristic is that religion is taking on new forms we don't fully grasp. That is why in the discussion above about principles, I used *belief system* rather than *religion*. Two important reasons for our current social divisiveness are (1) the change itself, and (2) a definition of religion that is inadequate for our time.

Religion, as the word is commonly used today in the United States and Europe, most often refers to traditional religions such as Christianity and Islam. When people speak of the decline of religion, they mean a move away from Christianity within those geographies. That is a fact. But two other facts are also important. Both Christianity and Islam are growing in other parts of the world. Furthermore, because of immigration, Islam is growing in parts of Europe. These facts are both true and obvious, and they have their own geopolitical significance. However, they represent only one of the major characteristics of belief systems for our time.

I think that the defining characteristic with regard to belief systems has two parts. First, our definition of religion is too narrow to capture what is happening now—thus, my use of *belief system*. Second, using the broader meaning of belief system, the implications of conflicting "doctrines" become more clear.

The earlier discussion of principles provided a broad definition of belief systems. Now, we need to look at the development of belief systems leading up to the present. As a reminder, the focus throughout this book when it comes to specifics is on the United States. However, it is natural that many of the details either apply to Europe today or were true of it in an earlier time.

The Cult of Reason, Marxism, communism, scientism, and syncretism are examples of belief systems. A detailed discussion of these examples is beyond the purpose of this book, but a few observations are useful. The Cult of Reason was an explicitly atheistic religion that took on trappings analogous to the Catholic Church in its effort to weaken or destroy Catholicism in France. Communism suppresses traditional belief systems in an attempt to make a new belief system integral with the rulership structure—in essence, a modern theocracy. Scientism, the weakest of the examples, is included because it is growing in its own right and because it is a common element of syncretism. Syncretism, of course, has been common throughout history. No single description of syncretism would accurately capture the mixture of beliefs present in the United States today. Nonetheless, it is useful to note some of the elements common to syncretic belief systems: Christianity (traditional and social), scientism, absolute personal autonomy, capitalism or socialism, and tenets of particular political parties.

What is important to see is that traditional religions are now just one among several belief systems impacting our society.

Until quite recently, Christianity has served explicitly as the underlying belief system for the United States, and because of its long history it remains the implicit bedrock. However, beginning early in the twentieth century, the various Christian churches began diverging on key beliefs. That divergence accelerated in recent decades such that disagreements among different Christian groups may be as intense as between Christian and non-Christian groups. Of course, there are always disagreements among different sects of a belief system, but those among Christian churches have reached a scope and intensity such that it is often not useful or clear to speak of *a* Christian belief system.

We need this more accurate understanding of belief systems in order to understand what is taking place in politics and public policy, because in those areas, the old categories are still used. That is, "religion" is used as a social and political category and is largely synonymous with Christianity. The United States is on a path already traveled by Europe and Canada in which the objective is to remove "religion" from all political and social discussion. However, because traditional religion is pervasive in the United States, attempts to remove it as an influence on public life is a major contributor to social divisiveness.

Recalling from the principles discussion above, all people hold a belief system, and one or more belief systems are always driving a society. Thus, removing "religion" from the public sphere is more properly understood as a contest among belief systems. Belief systems that are predominantly based on traditional Christian beliefs are being replaced by belief systems with other foundations. It is not possible to have political and public policy devoid of belief systems. One or more belief systems are always in play.

This process is following a plan commonly seen in history. Proponents of belief systems try to gain influence or control of government in order to subdue or eliminate competing belief systems. Especially in the United States where freedom is a deeply held and pervasive value, any efforts by the rulership structure to favor one belief system over another, and especially to displace the historically dominant belief system, is bound to generate divisiveness.

Throughout this book, we will be studying what happens when competing economic interests and competing belief systems attempt to gain control of the rulership structure for the purpose of gaining an advantage over the competition or, in some cases, eliminating the competition. These two domains, economics and belief systems, are integrated; they cannot be separated.

Part II

ANALYSIS AND SYNTHESIS

"If a nation expects to be ignorant and free, in a state of civilization, it expects what never was and never will be."
Thomas Jefferson

"Whoever would overthrow the liberty of a nation must begin by subduing the freeness of speech."
Benjamin Franklin

Part II

ANALYSIS AND SYNTHESIS

THINKING LIKE A RULER

"As citizens of this democracy, you are the rulers and the ruled, the law-givers and the law-abiding, the beginning and the end."
Adlai Stevenson I

"Nothing is more wonderful than the art of being free, but nothing is harder to learn how to use than freedom."
Alexis de Tocqueville

We as citizens must assume more responsibility as citizen-rulers. The implicit bargain that developed in the middle part of the last century assumed citizens could hand off the governing of the nation to elected officials who would work with experts to create and maintain an environment in which all citizens could flourish. That bargain has failed. The solution is not to attempt to assign blame either for the general failure or for the failure of specific policies. Rather, let us recognize that responsibility is shared by everyone: citizens, elected officials, and experts. If we want to remain a free and prosperous nation, the solution must come from citizen-rulers—a fact rooted in the very foundations of democracy.

What does this mean? For starters, it does not mean that we need to radically change the core structures and principles upon which the country was founded. Nor does it mean that we don't need experts both inside and outside of government, or that we do not need government agencies. All of these remain necessary. Furthermore, it does not mean that if only we could elect a great president our problems could be solved. Likewise, the solution does not lie in granting super majorities to a particular political party. The solution requires something more basic.

Citizens must equip themselves to be rulers, but rulers in a world that is more complex and more difficult than that of the mid-twentieth century. This increased complexity came about for two reasons. First, almost every component of our world is larger, more specialized, and more integrated as a natural result of freedom and increasing prosperity. That would be challenging enough. But secondly, the implicit bargain noted above brought about structural changes in politics, economics, and society. Although some of those changes are good, some are the basis of our problems today. Both of those drivers of increased complexity contributed to a very integrated system. As a result, we cannot address one specific problem at a time. Such an approach is more likely to cause damage than to bring about improvement. Rather than looking for independent solutions, we must first understand and then modify some of our fundamental models, assumptions, and implied contracts. In addition to the increase in complexity, our task is more difficult because the rate of change has been incredibly fast and getting faster. This is new territory for citizens, elected officials, and experts alike.

The ultimate power and therefore the ultimate responsibility for bringing about solutions resides with the citizenry. This means that we need to change our understanding so that we can make new and better assessments and act in new and better ways. This book is my contribution to proper understanding for the purpose of citizen assessments and citizen actions.

We need to first understand and then change a basic assumption behind the implicit bargain. As discussed earlier, coming out of World War II, many people believed that government, economic, and social policies could be developed and implemented using "scientific management." This belief was largely based on the economic successes of large corporations and the successful military operations associated with the war. We now know that those models are not applicable to the ongoing functioning of a free society.

A corollary of the basic assumption was that laws and regulations could be effectively used to not only shape but control the outcome of policies. Today, the number of government regulations has been estimated around 300,000. Each time a regulation fails or is circumvented, more regulations are added in an attempt to regain control. The failure of this approach is now clear from two perspectives. First, we have experiential evidence. Two examples will be briefly noted. Regulations tend to benefit large companies over small ones. Large companies have the resources to work around regulations and to use them as a competitive advantage. Second, some of our problems are partly caused by regulations, an example of which is the 2008 recession. The second perspective comes from the recognition that society is not a mechanical system but rather resembles a complex adaptive system. Both theory and experiments of smaller, simpler complex systems demonstrate that such systems cannot be controlled by imposing constraints (regulations).

To be clear, the above discussion is not arguing that government regulations are not necessary—they are. What is key is using them differently.

The lesson is this: the assumption that society can be "scientifically managed" to produce desired results is not a valid foundation for the governance of a free society. What then should replace the old framework? It requires a return to fundamental principles applied with wisdom to a modern democracy. Yes, wisdom, a word not often used today in public policy. Wisdom is necessary for applying principles to a particular society with particular circumstances. Wisdom includes humility, a recognition that perfect applications are not possible and that no person or group possesses perfect knowledge.

This new arrangement demands more responsibility from the individual citizen. An analogy may be helpful. The implicit bargain could be compared to a group of people who purchased a company and hired a management team to run it, with the expectation of continual growth in earnings and value. The new owners were aware that they did not know the technology or the company's processes. But the management team was convincing that they did understand the business and, furthermore, had access to any needed expertise. Along the way, the owners made some demands of the management team, unaware that their demands would motivate the management team to make changes and concessions that would damage the long-term outlook for the company. Even so, the owners were often disappointed and responded by replacing one management team after another.

Finally, after many years of repeating this pattern, the owners recognized that their company was in serious trouble. The owners lashed out at all members of the management team, present and past, as well as the various experts who had advised them. In addition, the owners attacked each other for having made poor decisions. Eventually, and fortunately, the owners acknowledged their responsibility as owners. They began to diligently study the principles and circumstances of their business and their industry. They developed better processes for selecting the management team and holding them accountable. Furthermore, because the management team made heavy use of experts and outside organizations, the owners developed means of assessing those groups also.

It took years of hard work and sacrifice for the owners to bring about those changes because even with better selection of management and experts, and better means of accountability, it took a long time to repair what was broken and to unwind what had been distorted within the company.

Citizens today are at a crisis point similar to where the owners of the company found themselves. We as citizens must take responsibility for fixing what is broken and restoring what is distorted. This requires not only more attention and effort but also the development of new knowledge and skills.

But there is another part of the story. Why did it take so long for the business owners to recognize what was happening? Where was the feedback that might have allowed the owners to take action earlier? Possibly, the information was available, but the owners were unwilling to invest the effort to understand it. Perhaps the owners didn't pay attention because they trusted the management team and had other things that needed their attention. Or maybe the management team, either through ignorance or deceit, did not create and deliver the information. Whatever the reasons, the owners as well as the enterprise, including employees, suffered due to the late intervention.

All of that applies to us as citizens, but it is more difficult for us than for the business owners because the functioning of a society is far more complicated than the functioning of a company. Recalling the discussion of *hard* and *soft* subjects in the first part of the book, much of what is important in society takes place in soft domains, in which it is both difficult to make assessments and the timespan between decisions and results might be decades. We thus find it more difficult to make assessments and decisions. Equally important because of the unique power held by government, multiple individuals and special interest groups will intentionally withhold or distort useful feedback information to influence government policy. Finally, a powerful but little-understood distortion arises from our monetary system. For these reasons, it is understandable why citizens did not take corrective action earlier.

However, more and more citizens now recognize the danger and the need for action. The task is first to understand how we got to this point, and second, to decide what must be done. The sequence is critical because if we try to solve problems without a proper understanding, we will only make things worse.

The first part of the book investigated principles valid for all time. For each principle, we looked at the characteristics of our present era. The principles and associated descriptions are prerequisite knowledge for citizens in our new role as citizen-rulers. It is not sufficient, however, because we must also understand concepts and circumstances particular to our time so that we can see and understand what is happening. That is, we need to be able to see and understand the feedback available to us so that we know how the principles are to be applied today. That is the objective of this part of the book.

We will begin by looking at the feedback-adjustment process in general, moving from simple, everyday examples to more subtle cases. The remaining chapters in this part will consider key structures in society for the purpose of developing an understanding proper to a citizen-ruler.

FEEDBACK, SELF-CORRECTING, DISTORTION

"A tree is straightened while it is still young."
African Proverb

"However beautiful the strategy, you should occasionally look at the results."
Winston Churchill

We rely on cause-effect relationships to learn, to act, and to understand our world generally. Without some degree of consistency between actions and results, between behaviors and consequences, the world would appear disordered, and productive human action would be difficult. This learning process can be generalized. We act or observe some action, we get feedback, we learn and adjust. In some cases, this process is clear, simple, and fast. However, things that matter most to the well-being of our society are often not clear or simple and take place over long periods of time. Furthermore, the feedback may be hidden or intentionally distorted. Thus, citizens must be informed and always vigilant in order to see and understand the feedback signals within society.

We will begin by reviewing a few simple, familiar examples of feedback and response. These examples can all be applied at a personal level. Of course, in this book, we are interested in the more complicated feedback and adjustment scenarios that occur in society. In assessing those more complicated cases, we struggle with grasping the feedback and coming up with good responses. In the middle portion of this chapter, we will briefly look at some of those challenges. Finally, we will review real social problems that parallel the simple examples. The purpose is to form a foundation for understanding the sometimes-subtle feedback and adjustment scenarios in upcoming chapters.

Consider the classic example of touching a hot stove. The feedback—the result or consequence—is pain, which results in the immediate adjustment of removing our hand from the hot object. This example is concrete and objective; in the language used earlier in the book, it is *hard*. That is, it is repeatable, unambiguous, and easily understood at each point of the process. Learning is fast and universal. In this example, we can reverse the consequences by removing our hand. We can learn without permanent damage.

In the next example, a person is walking along the edge of a cliff known to be dangerous when a small crumbling of the edge causes them to lose their balance and fall to their death on the rocks below. As in the first example, the results of falling off the cliff are clear, fast, and unambiguous. However, for the actor, there is no feedback, no lesson learned, and no chance of reversing the consequence. The feedback and learning belong to those who observe the event. The issue of reversibility turns into one of reducing future risks, maybe by posting warning signs or building a fence along the edge.

For our next example, feedback is intentionally distorted. Animals can learn to do an impressive set of actions to obtain a reward. The classic example is a rat learning a maze in order to receive a treat.

Likewise, animals learn to avoid painful situations, such as having one portion of an enclosed area deliver an electric shock if they step on it. But this learning is possible only if the environment to be mastered remains consistent. If the maze is continuously changed or if the treat at the end of the maze is sometimes there and sometimes not, the animal may become agitated or simply give up. Similarly, if the electrified locations of the cage are constantly changing, the animal may become paralyzed. In extreme cases, animals can even give up and die. Here, the feedback is not clear and unambiguous because an outside agent, the researcher, can change conditions and information at will.

Another type of action-feedback-adjustment scenario is characterized by a large time delay between initial feedback as information and much later feedback as consequences. The delay comes not because the final result cannot be known but because the ultimate expression of the feedback does not have to be dealt with until an endpoint arrives. In fact, the progress of the feedback may be observable over time but can be ignored for many years, perhaps decades. The development of a child is a common example for this type. It is well-known that proper training of a child greatly increases the chance that they will be a productive citizen as an adult. However, this training requires proper circumstances and much effort. Therefore, it is sometimes neglected or done poorly. The adjustment or response will then come at a later stage and may take the form of a poor quality of life for the individual or as a liability or menace for society.

In our final type, the feedback (result) from an action is not known, and often cannot be known, until many years or decades later. Smoking cigarettes is an example. The product was not created with the intent to damage the health of smokers. However, eventually the clinical and scientific evidence proved that smoking was a major public health danger. At that point, the adjustment process (the response) consisted of two primary actions: first, learning to treat the resultant diseases, and second, discouraging the practice of smoking. While we can improve our ability to look into the future, this type of greatly delayed feedback is unavoidable in our rapidly changing world.

The examples above are simple and easy to grasp. Each represents a type of feedback-adjustment that is applicable throughout our social, economic, and political lives. Today, many of the problems generating great concern are the result of not seeing or understanding feedback information, being deceived by distorted feedback, or failing to make corrective adjustments to feedback. The following problems, for instance, have all reached their current state as a result of poor execution of the feedback-adjustment process: inadequate education, economic inequality, unaffordable medical care, substance abuse, housing shortage, high debt, and underfunded retirement. As citizens who want to regain rulership control, we need to understand how these problems came about and how to begin corrective action.

When we turn attention from the simple, personal examples above to what we encounter as citizens, what is required in order to first recognize and interpret feedback and second to respond effectively? First, we must know where to pay attention. In the previous chapter, using the analogy of an owner of a company, we saw that assumptions in the implicit bargain between rulership and citizens proved to be false. Citizens must pay far more attention and take far more responsibility than assumed in that earlier worldview. Freedom, prosperity, and peace are not natural. Like a garden, they require constant attention and maintenance lest the natural state of disorder take over. In fact, the more highly developed a society and the greater the benefits it offers its citizens, the more vigilance is required.

Vigilance alone, however, is not sufficient. We also require a proper worldview, a knowledge of principles and of the particular structures, processes, and institutions of our society. In the first part of the book, we considered fundamental principles. In this part we will look at some of the particulars of our society. In the following part, we will bring those together and apply them in some detail to current social problems. Through all of this, the first goal is to learn to see and understand what is happening, which includes looking for feedback that is not obvious and recognizing feedback that is distorted. The second goal is to use that feedback to formulate and execute an effective response, that is, to adjust to what has been learned. The balance of this chapter will be devoted to the broad challenges in achieving those two goals.

Perhaps our biggest challenge comes from the many new things that happened so quickly following World War II and which continue to the present. Although we discussed some of these previously, it is worth a quick review. We often think of the new world order following World War II in geopolitical terms. However, the social and economic order of almost every country was also restructured. In the free world, the following things increased rapidly: population, longevity, wealth, and freedom. Newly developing economic and social structures interacted with each other, further accelerating change. Those new realities, in turn, brought about new types of decisions in every domain of our lives: economic, family, education, health, technology, and social relationships. For the first time in history the majority of citizens in a society no longer had to worry about a basic standard of living. They could pursue those motivations higher up Maslow's hierarchy. As a society, we did not keep up with all of these new things; we did not understand and therefore did not adjust along the way.

Information, which is a specific form of feedback, also grew rapidly. The impact of information was so important that beginning in the middle of the twentieth century the moniker "The Information

Age" became popular. Today, the flow of information itself has been blamed for social and political problems. The next chapter is dedicated to this subject.

What is less often discussed is a reduction in important, traditional forms of feedback. The nature of family and community underwent changes that eventually led to their breakdown for some citizens. Intermediate institutions, most notably churches and schools, changed in ways that negated much of their feedback and guidance, and that which was not negated was often confused and conflicted. The vacuum formed by the loss of feedback from family and intermediate institutions was gradually filled by other sources such as social media and the entertainment industry.

Government in general, and especially the federal government, continued to gain power at an unprecedented peacetime rate. As the influence of government touched every domain of life, it changed the types of feedback, the interpretation of feedback, and the options available for responding to feedback. These things presented challenges to all citizens but especially to the ordinary citizen, that is to those who were far removed from the center of power.

One of the things that enabled the federal government to dramatically expand its power was yet another new thing: a new type of world monetary system. As we will see in a later chapter, there have, in fact, been two monetary systems since World War II. The current monetary system, which we will study in a later chapter, not only changes the nature of feedback but distorts it in ways that are little appreciated. Again, the complications arising from this feedback tend to work to the disadvantage of the common citizen.

Few issues we face in society have the obvious and quick feedback we get from touching a hot object. But there are approximations, an example of which is price controls. A common instance of price control is city-based rent control. Over decades, cities have experimented with imposing rent controls, supposedly for the benefit of providing affordable housing. In each case, the result has been a reduced supply of rental housing, along with a reduced quality of such housing. Yet, at the time of this writing, a major United States city voted to impose rent control regulations. Almost immediately, developers began withdrawing building permits. That is, a fast response followed the feedback (information) from the voters. Why, in the face of overwhelming evidence about the negative outcomes that will result, would a city vote to impose rent controls? Perhaps it is because it feels like "doing something" when no one is willing to do the harder work to fix what caused the housing problem in the first place. Perhaps it is because the worst of the outcomes will not be obvious for a number of years. Whatever the reason, this is a good example of why, when dealing with social situations, we often don't learn even when consequences follow swiftly and with great impact.

Two points are important to highlight here. One has to do with the extent to which the consequences of an action can be reversed. At a personal level, we can all think of numerous cases in which consequences cannot be reversed. However, at a social level, the problems of most interest are those that may be reversed but only with great effort and a long time, and even then the reversal may only be partial. The second point is that some of the most valuable lessons come from observing the consequences of the actions of others. Their consequences serve as feedback for us. A good illustration began in 1999 and continues to the time of this writing. The citizens of Venezuela were dissatisfied with their circumstances and responded by electing the socialist Hugo Chavez (whose policies were followed by his successor Nicolas Maduro).

Soon after his election, Chavez began his promised agenda of socialism. The negative impact on the economic structure of the country played out over the following years but was largely masked due to the rising price of oil, on which Venezuela is very dependent. In fact, for a while it appeared the country was making real progress. However, when the price of oil dropped, the economic damage from his policies was visible. Presently, Venezuelans are suffering in multiple ways. Many are poor, hungry, and sick. For several years, they suffered triple-digit rates of inflation, and those who had the means left the country. It has been assessed as a failed state. Why would the citizens have voted for this future? Many examples in the twentieth century had already proven the failure of socialist governments and central planning. Yet, amazingly, the citizens ignored those lessons. It appears there is something in human nature that makes it difficult for us to learn from the lessons of others. Maybe someday we can compensate for that weakness and learn to avoid unnecessary suffering.

The third example was about distorted feedback. Relative to the experimental animal, the researcher was powerful and could be as arbitrary as desired. Likewise, to distort social feedback requires power. Feedback that is important in society can be distorted through deception, intentional manipulation, and systemic effects. In the next chapter we will see how powerful information companies can distort the flow of feedback. The most powerful of organizations, the federal government, has increasingly been willing to intentionally distort information flow to citizens through omission and deception. The deception may come through what is said or through the altering of data. However, as long as citizens have complete freedom, including freedom of speech, those two illustrations can be discovered and circumvented by vigilant and knowledgeable citizens.

But it is much more difficult to see and respond to distorted feedback coming from systemic government policy. The policies that produce the distortion typically come about because the government is acting in response to what citizens want and have expressed through their political, economic, and social voting. The distortion is an unintended consequence of a purposeful policy. However, the distortion does not completely conceal the feedback or the ultimate results. Careful analysis by a knowledgeable person using fundamental principles would reveal the significance of the ongoing feedback and would also show the final consequences. Rather, the effect of the distortion is twofold. It postpones by decades the realization of ultimate outcomes, thus making it easy to postpone action. Second, the mitigating effects of the distortion causes some people to doubt if the final consequences will really materialize. "This time is different" is an easy-to-induce mindset in modernity.

All of the major social problems which are approaching crisis status today have at least partly come about because of this type of feedback distortion. A few examples include policies directed at affordable housing, universal education, reduction of poverty, and economic expansion. Today, more and more citizens are frustrated, anxious, and confused because no solutions are forthcoming—and the problems are worsening. The resulting social and political conflict and divisiveness is the social analog to the frustrated, confused animal in the experiment in the original simple example.

Our next example also deals with a long time delay between the beginning and end of the feedback response process. There is an important distinction between this example and the one above in which distortion caused confusion and partially concealed what was really happening. In our present example, the progression from feedback as information to feedback as consequence is known but does not demand a definite action until the end of the process. In our initial simple example, we looked at the process of child development from infancy to young adult. We could have used other illustrations such as financial planning for retirement or taking care of our long-term health. In each illustration, it is common knowledge what the likely outcomes will be if children are not trained, if retirement financial planning is not followed, or if we live unhealthy lifestyles.

Why is it useful to separate the distortion example from this present one? Both of them result in a consequence, a problem that must be dealt with many years later. Both shift real costs from the present to the future, which often means from one group of citizens to another. Yet, there are significant differences that will influence how we address the problems in the short-term and what we do to correct the long-term process.

Distorted feedback tends to create society-wide problems by altering the development of economic, political, and social structures. The entire society is caught up in the results of the distortion. It is different when we consider examples in which the progression is knowable. The resulting problems are more likely to be characterized as a failure of personal responsibility—that is, when a person didn't do what they should have to avoid the future consequences. Thus, there will be some tendency to say that the person must bear the consequences personally. However, because of the ways in which our society is structured, these "personal problems" will always have an impact on other citizens.

While paying attention to personal responsibility is important and will become more important in the years ahead, it is a mistake to think that these problems are totally driven by insufficient personal responsibility. The structures that develop under distorted feedback are such that it is very difficult for many citizens to properly respond to a knowable feedback-response scenario even if they are motivated to do so. In the chapters ahead where we will look at inequality, education, and economics, we will see why this is true. Those later discussions will make the somewhat abstract discussion here much more concrete and specific.

Unknowable future consequences was the last of our simple examples. Rapid advances in science and technology over the past 100 years have made a particular type of action-feedback process more important to society than it was a couple of hundred years ago. Some actions have consequences (feedback) that may not be known until decades later. In the simple example, this was illustrated by cigarette smoking. Many other illustrations could come from manufacturing processes, use of chemicals, and medical technology. On balance and up to this time, the benefits to our quality of life have exceeded the negative consequences. But negative consequences continue to accumulate. Furthermore, the challenge has become more difficult as a result of new types of science and technology breakthroughs, examples of which include genetic engineering and so-called "artificial intelligence." These technologies have the potential to alter human life and society. Extremely important decisions will be made within the next decade or two.

Even if we wished to do so, it is not possible to stop scientific and technological progress. The moral, biological, and social consequences of these new things will likely demand a faster, broader response from society than was necessary to accommodate the changes of last century. New thinking and new responses will be required because these new technologies have the potential to change the world more dramatically and more quickly than did most previous changes.

This chapter took as a starting point what we saw in the first part of the book. Effective human action requires a world that is ordered and consistent in both physical and natural laws. Otherwise, the action-feedback-adjustment process is meaningless. But the process requires more than that; it requires possessing the knowledge necessary to understand the feedback and to formulate a productive response. We cannot survive, let alone thrive, without the capability for productive feedback and response.

The purpose of this chapter was to provide a foundation for the remainder of the book. This was accomplished by looking at several types of feedback-adjustment examples, first in simple and personal terms, and later expanded to a social context. In between, we sketched a number of impediments for citizens seeing and understanding feedback information, and also for citizens formulating an effective response to the feedback. Over the next several chapters, we will study the knowledge necessary to see, understand, and respond.

INFORMATION STRUCTURE

"Few traits of totalitarian regimes are at the same time so confusing to the superficial observer and yet so characteristic of the whole intellectual climate as the complete perversion of language."
F.A. Hayek

"If language is not correct, then what is said is not what is meant; if what is said is not what is meant, then what must be done remains undone ... Hence there must be no arbitrariness in what is said. This matters above everything."
Confucius

We have more data, more tools for data analysis, and more information available to us than ever before. Why then do we have to work harder to make decisions for our personal lives? Why are social problems becoming more difficult to solve rather than easier? And more recently, why has information itself become a matter of social conflict? If we are to be citizen-rulers, we must try to answer these questions.

So often we have heard that we live in an age of information and knowledge that it is easy to overlook what that really means. Much of the standard of living we enjoy today is the result of the application of knowledge, which in turn allows the development of yet more knowledge. In addition, our world is large, dispersed, integrated, and specialized. All of these demand the flow of information. In free countries, information is the primary means of influence politically, socially, and economically. Stated simply, information is influence.

A common assessment today is that our struggles with information are due to an increasing need for information at the same time that the volume of information is growing so fast that we can't keep up. Furthermore, information is becoming more unreliable and sometimes deceitful. In response, some people suggest that we can develop more sophisticated and more powerful tools to process data and information so that we can more easily make better decisions. Others call for regulation of information to ensure that what we receive is truthful and useful. Perhaps some benefit will come from those ideas, but neither will make our struggles go away, and both approaches present additional risks to our use of information. For real help, we require a more fundamental understanding of information and its evaluation.

In this chapter, I use *information* to mean a communication that has been created for the purpose of influencing the thinking and decisions of other people. Examples include statements by a government official, the content of a television news show, an opinion piece in a newspaper, and a posting on social media. This is the type of information we use daily and that influences social, political, and economic decisions—that is, our voting as citizens. It is also this type of information those in power wish to control.

Much of what gets our attention and shapes our thinking are small pieces of information such as a short web or magazine article, a video clip, or a social media posting. This information is often prepared by a single person or a small group working on their own or employed by large, influential organizations yet capable of creating and propagating information as if they were independent. Examples include college professors, business executives, and government officials. Some particularly important exceptions to the "small group" qualifier are television channels, Internet news channels, and national periodical publications. This type of source not only propagates information produced by other smaller sources but also creates their own.

We will look at three aspects of our information environment. First is the information itself: what we see and hear, what was purposefully created by someone in the hope of influencing others. Next, we will consider the use and meaning of words, a subject often neglected today but which is of utmost importance. Finally, we will examine the control of information, something which has recently become significant and contentious.

Information: Volume and Quality

We will consider several questions: Why has the volume of information available to us become so large so quickly? Why has it become less reliable? Why has some of it become outright deceitful, and in what ways has it become so?

Technology has enabled the volume of information. Only in recent years have all of the parts come together so that it is inexpensive and easy to publish information. It was not so many years ago that to publish a book you had to go to a publishing company, and to create a useful website you needed to find an expert. Today, almost anyone can do either one of those things on their own and at little expense. Social media platforms provide a mechanism to instantaneously present information and opinion. Money, expertise, and credibility are no longer limiting factors.

The reduced reliability or quality of information is caused by two changes, both of which are tied to the volume of information, as discussed above. Presenting information using the older communication mechanisms was more time-consuming and expensive, but those mechanisms had a built-in vetting process. Due to the required investment of time and expense, everyone in the process worked to ensure a return on their investment. Likewise, most information was produced in tangible form such as paper or film, which created a permanent record that connected the information with the organization that published it. This, in turn, created accountability through a desire to maintain reputation and avoid liability. Of course, that older system didn't guarantee reliable information, and it certainly shut out much that would have been useful had it been published. Nonetheless, it represented some control, whereas today's channels of communication provide no vetting of information at all. Both the competent and incompetent have equal access to communication platforms.

This reality does not suggest that people should be prevented from communicating; it simply means that consumers of information must do their own assessment to filter out sloppy or incompetent sources.

We face a more serious and difficult problem when a source of information is deceitful. Here, we will focus on cases in which individuals or groups who, given their positions, roles, or responsibilities, should be credible but decide to use their standing to put out false and misleading information.

We are accustomed to elected officials and those running for election being less than truthful and intentionally ambiguous in what they say. However, until recent years, most of the public had a higher level of confidence in information coming from (non-elected) government agencies. Today, however, it is increasingly common to catch officials from such agencies behaving like elected politicians, saying one thing and doing another, or knowingly giving false information. Likewise, science, which once enjoyed a high level of public confidence, has produced many examples of false or politicized information. As a result, the public is rapidly losing trust in sources they once saw as credible. This diminished trust is damaging to a free society.

As citizens, we must ask why this breakdown in trust is happening. A common answer is a decline in morality, but that is true by definition and therefore not helpful. I suggest there are a couple of reasons. The drive for power, influence, and favor related to anything associated with government, and especially the federal government, is strong and getting stronger. As a result, some leaders in companies, universities, research labs, media, and nonprofits are more willing to distort reality or to be deceitful in order to line up with government thinking.

Second, over the past couple of decades, the impact of social causes and agendas and of political polarity have become important forces. Some people who strongly support a particular cause, agenda, or political view believe that what they support is so important that any means is justified to advance their purpose. For such zealots, giving deceitful information is not a violation of ethics or morality but is, in fact, the right thing to do.

Before considering the use and meaning of words, I want to briefly deal with the subject of images. Photographs and videos constitute a much larger percentage of the information we consume than was true a few decades ago. Technology to alter images has become quite sophisticated. Altering photographs, of course, is not new. It has been done almost as long as photography has existed. What is new is that technology allows the altering of photographs in ways that could never be done before and that the average person cannot discern. Thus, a photograph may appear to represent something that never existed nor happened.

The same things can be said about videos. A video can be edited to convey events that didn't happen. Videos, however, need special consideration because of quite recent technology that allows real-time altering. This technology will soon advance such that what is purported to be a live video of some event will, in fact, be a mixture of what is actually happening plus computer-generated changes. Such technology will be used deceitfully.

What is essential for citizens to know is that we can no longer judge video images by the maxim, "Seeing is believing." This means images have to be validated analogously to written material. Ultimately, the only sure method of verifying information may be to have a trusted source who was actually present attest to the authenticity. This presents a threat in a free society.

Use and Meaning of Words

We communicate through, and react to, words, images, and actions. However, to think, to reason, and to communicate precisely requires words. If the meaning of a word or term is confused, corrupted, or understood differently among concerned parties, communication will be ineffective and will likely result in undesirable conclusions and decisions.

Words are especially important today. Our complex and dispersed-yet-integrated world requires a great deal of coordinating information. Our age is one of ideas and concepts that must be carefully communicated and understood. In a free country, citizens are always under "attack" by those who want to use words to gain power. Free citizens must be always vigilant in the use of language, both by themselves and by others.

Words and terms may have two types of meaning: a literal meaning, which is the dictionary definition or denotation, and a connotation, which is the implicit meaning brought about by ideas or feelings associated with the word or term. (Hereafter, I will use *word* to mean both word and term.) For example, the word "home" has an obvious literal meaning but may also connote warmth, belonging, and comfort. Both types of meaning are important in communication. For some words, the connotation may carry more weight than the denotation. The two components of meaning may change independently.

The meaning of words can change or become confused through a natural process arising from common usage or through an intentional, agenda-driven process. The natural process happens when a word is repeatedly used imprecisely in reference to ideas, events, and circumstances which are, in fact, different. This often happens when it would take extra effort to carefully qualify the use of a word to more accurately fit a specific context. The agenda-driven process happens when a group decides that changing or confusing the meaning of a word would be helpful in advancing a social, economic, or political goal. An intentional effort rarely begins with changing the literal meaning; rather, it begins by working to change the connotations associated with the word. Another approach is to extend the meaning of a word beyond its traditional usage. These points are more easily seen with examples.

Democracy is often used to simply mean a country that holds elections, regardless of whether its beliefs and institutions can support such freedom. At the other extreme, democracy is used to mean everything that makes the American system work: its government structure, formal and informal institutions, economic structure, and culture. In countries that are not free, a third meaning of democracy is the perceived benefits in the United States, namely, freedom and prosperity. The connotations of democracy are not always positive. In recent decades, some countries have tried "democracy" and were unhappy with the results. In such a country, *democracy* now has a negative connotation even though democracy in its fullest sense was never present in the country. The development of a negative connotation was, of course, fully supported by people in those countries who wanted to gain more power.

Capitalism. What was said about democracy applies for capitalism also. But it goes further. The United States is often seen as the paradigmatically capitalist country. Yet even within the United States, *capitalism* means quite different things to different groups. A good example of the confusion that can arise from incompatible meanings was seen clearly following the economic downturn of 2008. Many people around the world, and many in the United States, saw this as a failure of capitalism. Yet there are understandings of *capitalism* that would have nothing to do with the mechanism that brought about that downturn. Nonetheless, in some countries there was a turning away from capitalism because it appeared to have failed.

The word *capitalism* also serves as an example of agenda-driven changes in meaning. In the United States, a small but growing number of people believe that capitalism is the cause of a number of our social problems. In that context, capitalism means the economic system in its totality. The solution, one which was explicitly advocated in the last presidential election, is to turn to socialism. However, *socialism* was also not carefully defined but was meant to mean not-capitalism. The agenda was to associate negative sentiment with capitalism and positive with socialism.

A few other words that are socially significant today and that are undergoing a confusion of meaning include *tolerance, freedom,* and *inequality.* They will not be expounded upon here but are discussed throughout the book.

Control of Information
History shows that at all times some people have attempted to suppress information and control the flow of information. The same is true

today. Those who wish to control and suppress information generally fall into two groups. The group that is most effective are those at the top of power structures who are motivated by the desire to gain and consolidate power. The second group are zealots for a particular cause, who believe that anyone who thinks differently should be suppressed.

We also learn from history that the methods of suppressing information and controlling its flow remain the same. The particular mechanisms depend upon time and place, but the essence remains. Three methods are common: remove people, destroy media, control the conduits.

For most of history, writing was the primary form of nonverbal communication, but the ability to produce multiple copies of written information was time-consuming and expensive. Thus, an effective means of suppressing information was to destroy written records and then kill or exile those who produced them. For those who created troubling information (usually ideas) but produced no writing, the solution was easy: kill or exile the creator. Independent conduits for information were not a major factor until recent centuries. In our day, however, those who wish to suppress and control information must combine all three methods.

Removing people remains an effective method. In many parts of the world, governments may imprison or assassinate those who disagree with current leaders or policies. In a subset of those countries, leaders of a belief system (religion) may have the same power. In that same subset, zealots, who are not part of the power structure, may also kill others judged as heretics. In free countries, those means of removing people are extremely rare and have been replaced with other methods. In the United States, the "remove people" method consists of threats to social standing, threats to economic well-being, and the threat of federal prosecution. People can lose their jobs or effectively be shut out of an industry if what they say or write does not line up with those who hold the relevant power. Governments can threaten to prosecute under laws dealing with discrimination or "hate speech." Local and state governments may attempt to prevent an organization from operating within their jurisdiction. Stated simply, physical violence has been replaced by social and economic coercion. In the United States, a new term has come into use: "canceled" means removing a person's influence by means other than killing or exile.

For those who want to suppress information and control its flow, the world is much different than fifty years ago and is of a whole different kind compared to 150 years ago. Controlling information by destroying its physical form—for example, by censoring and burning books—is no longer viable. Technological advances in computing, communications, and software have made the conduits of information far more important from a control standpoint. At this time, in fact, these conduits are probably the most important target for control. Debate today centers on the fact that a few extremely large companies hold powerful control in social media, Internet searches, smart phone apps, distribution of books, and "cloud-based" computing and information storage, all of which are central to the distribution of information.

In recent years, those companies have been both criticized and praised for their behavior related to "fake news" and to their censoring of information flow related to political elections, social issues, science, and public health. Some people can speak freely through these channels while others are prohibited. Some can distribute their books while others cannot. Some applications and videos are permitted, others are not. And so on. The leaders of those companies may be motivated by two reasons. They may have a social or political agenda they want to support by controlling information, or they may be responding to social or political pressure from powerful groups. In either case, the manner in which they are controlling information has added more fuel to the political and social polarity and contention.

The most important thing to remember is that the current configuration exists because citizens, by their economic and social voting, have made it possible. Companies become huge and powerful because they offer something people want, and people purchase from them. If citizens believe such power is being abused, they have at least two paths to change it. One is to change their economic votes; the other is to appeal to government.

This problem involves important principles. On the one side, those large information companies are privately owned, and private companies have the right to conduct their business as they think appropriate. As such, they have the right to restrict who their clients are and decide which products they want to provide or not to provide. These, and other operational decisions, are taken for granted by both large and small companies. On the other side, the companies have become so large and dominant that they may require special attention from the government. Interestingly, many people—on both sides of the political divide—who have offered ideas and solutions want the government to act; they simply have different views of what the right government action should be.

When principles are at stake, citizen-rulers must think carefully about any change, considering broader and longer-term implications than just the immediate problem. For example, if government is given the right to tell a handful of companies how to conduct their business, it is clear from experience that government will continually expand the number of companies for which intervention seems justifiable. This will turn into another avenue for government to increase power.

Proposed solutions involve government officials making the same type of decisions now made by the company officials. That is, there would still be a group of people deciding which citizens can have accounts, what books can be published, and so on. The risks of this approach should be obvious: the regulating body would soon become a tool for government officials to use for increased power.

In the spirit of this book, I don't presume to offer the right solution. Rather, I will offer ideas for consideration, ideas I think are consistent with the goal of citizens regaining more influence over power structures. Consider a thought experiment in which, overnight, one-half of the customers of one of these large companies simply quit doing business with it. Two things are likely to happen. First, that company would scramble to figure out what it needed to change in order to get back the customers who left. Second, if the company could not or would not respond effectively, a competitor would step in, after which there would no longer be a single dominant player. Of course, this is simplistic, but the point is valid. Companies respond to economic voting. From the perspective of freedom and citizen-rulers, a split driven by the economic votes of citizens is preferable to a split dictated by government.

Approaching the problem from another direction, these large companies feel pressure in both directions. Some people want to hold them accountable if they allow distribution of communication perceived as damaging to society. The obvious problem with this is the company cannot win because in a divided country there are large groups of people with directly opposing ideas of what is beneficial and harmful. The company can find itself caught between two determined groups and in some cases between two conflicting legal liabilities. Therefore, an acceptable solution does not seem likely if the burden is placed on the company.

That conundrum highlights an important question of principle. Should some group in a society, whether government, private institutions, or others, control the information available to the rest of society? Some people believe strongly that society should be protected and guided by controlling what information is available. Others believe equally strongly that information should not be controlled and that free citizens must judge information for themselves. From the principles of power discussed in the first part of the book, we know that any group given the power to control information will use it to further their power. On the other hand, a fair case can be made that, on occasion, large groups of citizens have misunderstood information and therefore made decisions detrimental to themselves or to society.

If we are again to assume the responsibility of citizen-rulers, we can't turn every problem over to a government solution. Because information is critical in our society, it is essential that citizens learn how to assess and use information. Part of that task is to develop proper understanding of principles, concepts, and practices. But there is too much information on too many specialized subjects for any one citizen to fully understand every issue that arises. I suggest that with proper understanding, citizens can make top-level assessments of issues and key pieces of information. It usually takes far less time to assess a situation using principles and concepts than it does to understand the technical details. Similarly, we need to assess leaders and experts based on principles. This greatly increases the chances of identifying competent, trusted leaders and experts.

ECONOMIC STRUCTURE

"So that the record of history is absolutely crystal clear, that there is no alternative way, so far discovered of improving the lot of the ordinary people that can hold a candle to the productive activities that are unleashed by the free-enterprise system."
Milton Friedman

In spite of hopeful predictions that economic striving would eventually take second place to higher ideals, all of history refutes that idea. Today our world is governed for ever-increasing economic production. In one way or another, most of the problems we face are assumed to have an economic basis. Although the standard of living for most of the world has never been better, anxiety around economic issues has never been higher. That is certainly true of the United States. Concerns about inequality, productivity, demographics, and social stability raise many questions and generate strongly conflicting opinions. Yet no solutions are in view. This is true because our economic structure does not conform to the principles presented in the first part of this book, nor is the structure adjusting in response to economic and social feedback.

The state of the economy—present and anticipated—drives more political votes than any other subject. Economic matters seem to be the center of focus in almost every social issue. Therefore, as citizens who want to regain control of the power structures, we must properly understand economics.

Why is economic understanding so often ignored or misguided? First, we have been led to believe that economics can only be understood with specialized training, and that it is a complicated subject governed entirely by mathematics. Second, economists consistently fail to correctly predict the economic future, often badly so. When economists attempt to explain what has happened, including why their predictions were wrong, they often disagree with each other, sometimes offering exactly opposite explanations. Third, what happens in the economy can appear unexplainable or unreasonable. An individual citizen may feel that their life is subject to the workings of an unknowable and unfair system. Thus, citizens may despair of understanding and may become angry at the government and other players. Because human nature drives us to possess some explanation of our world, we may develop simplistic—and incorrect—views of how the economy works.

Fortunately, it is possible for the average person to understand economics. It is not a *hard* science as is physics, for example. It cannot be reduced to mathematics, experiments cannot be reproduced, and there is not a single, verifiably correct answer to problems. Economics is better understood as a study in sociology than as a mathematical science. In fact, one reason predictions are often wrong is that they are made with mathematical models. Specialized economic training is absolutely not necessary for citizens to make well-informed decisions.

There was a time, say, 150 years ago, when what a citizen needed to know about economics was acquired as "common sense" as part of daily life. This is no longer true. Over the past 100 years our economic structure has become increasingly complicated and distorted. Therefore, citizens must now intentionally pursue economic understanding.

Free markets are a natural part of a free society. Much of what we need to know about free markets flows easily from the principles discussed in the first part of the book. Understanding the source and nature of the distortions present in our economic structure and processes is not as simple, however. It is largely these distortions that create unnecessary problems and unfairness in society. Both the citizenry and government officials want to explain such distortions by pointing to one or maybe a few causes. But that is not reality. The distortions are the result of multiple big changes that have occurred in society, government, and our monetary structure over the past seventy years. And these changes have continuously interacted with each other to produce our present social and economic structures. Much of this book is directed at explaining those changes and their implications.

Because economics is of unique importance, it is addressed throughout this book by explaining concepts and mechanisms and by giving examples and applications. While it is true that our economic structure is complex, no complicated theories or mathematics are required. Every citizen has the capacity to understand our economic structure well enough to make informed votes, not only economically but socially and politically. In this chapter, we look at how the principles and characteristics presented in earlier chapters are manifested in our economy today.

As we will explore in an upcoming chapter, the economic structure of our society is partly the result of our monetary structure. Some of the problems with our current economic structure, problems that are an important part of political debate today, would not exist or would be greatly mitigated under a different monetary structure. To offer just one example, we have been accustomed to ever-increasing prices. Stated differently, we are accustomed to the dollar continuously losing purchasing power. However, under a different monetary structure, increasing productivity would result in decreasing prices. In this chapter, however, we are talking about the economic structure as it is today.

Prices and Production

In a free economy, consumers decide what will be produced and what price will be paid. Many people have this understanding backward because, to any one person, it appears that both the goods available and their prices are determined by the producer, but consumers operating in the marketplace will determine the price.

This can be seen by working through a simple example. Before a company decides to produce a new product, it researches the cost of production and the likelihood that consumers want the product and will pay a price that yields a profit. If the company has judged correctly, everyone benefits. Consumers get a product they want and the company makes a profit. It is possible, however, that the company misjudged the price that consumers were willing to pay. If so, the company will have to reduce the price to a level agreeable to customers. If that price turns out to be too low, the company will discontinue production of the product.

Consumers cannot ensure that a certain product will be available at a certain price. They simply make a decision of what they are willing to pay for a product. Let's look at how this might play out by assuming in the example above that the original company decided they would quit production because consumers were unwilling to pay the needed price. A second company might recognize that consumers indeed want the product but are only willing to pay a price that is 50 percent of what the first company required. Furthermore, the second company learns that consumers would be okay with some adjustments to the features and quality. The second company does additional research that allows them to produce a product that does essentially the same thing and that can be offered at the new, lower price. Here, it is clear how consumers have determined the price.

The only time a company can truly set the price for a good or service is if two conditions are met. First, what it provides must be a necessity for the normal life of consumers. Second, the government must grant the company a monopoly that prevents competitors from entering that particular market. Unless both of those conditions are true, the process is subject to the desires of consumers and to market competition as described above.

Thus, we see how consumers as a group control production and pricing, even though to any particular consumer both the array of products being offered and their prices appear to be unchangeable. This is the primary way consumers cast economic votes. They decide if they will purchase something and at what price they will do so. From those votes, the production structure of society is largely determined.

Measurement of Production and Inflation

Measurements of economic production and inflation are fundamental measurements used by the Federal Reserve and government in determining policies. The measurements affect government budget, taxes, and the target for interest rates. As a result, they have a direct impact on the quality of lives of citizens. Therefore, it is essential that citizen-rulers have a good conceptual understanding of what these measurements represent and how they are calculated.

The measurements are not straightforward and unambiguous. In fact, the officially reported numbers are not direct measurements but are rather the result of many assumptions and adjustments applied to actual measurements. In broad terms, the process looks like this: (1) based on assumptions in economic models, actual measurements of prices and purchases are obtained from within the economy, (2) those actual measurements are then processed in the economic models, which have multiple assumptions and adjustments set according to the judgment of the people running the models, (3) the output of the models is various numbers representing economic production and inflation. That is, there is not a single number representing either measurement. However, production and inflation each have a primary number, which will be the focus in this chapter.

The economic production of a country is typically represented by gross domestic product (GDP). A simplified definition of GDP is the sum of expenditures on finished goods and services. As noted earlier in the book, it is reasonable to say that the world is governed for growth in GDP. This remains true today, even though no one would claim that GDP is the ultimate measure of quality of life. It is, however, a single number and one that government can easily influence.

Some simple examples will serve to illustrate how GDP can increase as a result of things that decrease the quality of life. Money spent to pay for the cost of war, natural disasters, and pandemics count in the GDP calculation. If some member of a family must reluctantly take a job in order to make ends meet, even at the expense of providing other care and services to the family, GDP will increase. If the cost of running the government goes up, so does GDP.

Inflation is a measure of increases in prices. The Consumer Price Index (CPI) is the value most often reported, but it also has a few common variants.

It is common to read or hear that the cost of living is going up faster than the CPI. Two things account for most of this discrepancy. The government assumes "a basket of goods and services" that is typical for the average person. To the extent that a particular person's actual consumption differs from that basket, their cost of living will be different also. Second, because politicians are judged by inflation, the government is motivated to justify lower values of the CPI. For example, subjective judgment is used in determining the quality of a good or service. If the price of something goes up by 5 percent but subjective opinion says the quality of the product increased by 5 percent, it is counted as if no inflation took place. Furthermore, the agency in charge of calculating the CPI can assume if the price of a particular good goes up, consumers will switch to a different product. This effectively changes the basket of goods. These examples are simplified but they convey the essence of what actually takes place.

Now that we have a grasp of what GDP and inflation are, we can look at how they are related. When the government calculates GDP, it begins by gathering current prices, that is, prices in today's dollars. But these prices need to be adjusted for inflation. Technically, the GDP is first computed in *nominal* terms, meaning in today's prices. Then it is *deflated* using some measure of inflation. Again, sticking with simple concepts, if nominal GDP increased by 3 percent from one year to the next, and if inflation also increased by 3 percent, then the real growth in GDP would be zero. Publicly reported GDP numbers are the real values, after reduced by inflation.

Because strong gains in GDP convey that the country is being run effectively, the government is motivated to make assumptions and adjustments that increase GDP and decrease inflation. Not only does an understated inflation rate bolster "real GDP," because inflation is tied to a number of automatic payments, it reduces what the government must spend.

In spite of the complications and inadequacies of the measures of GDP and inflation, they are not likely to change in the near future. As citizens, the information presented here is primarily useful in understanding what is happening and what is reported. It is also useful in explaining why our personal experience may differ considerably from reported numbers. Finally, understanding the background behind these two fundamental measurements helps us understand other measurements derived from them.

Growth and Productivity

Setting aside the technical and political issues associated with measurement, we can look at essential concepts underlying economic growth and productivity. Our economic structure of production would work fine even if no government measurements were estimated. To emphasize that point, GDP won't be used in this portion of the chapter. Also, in order to focus on the essential concepts, we will assume there are no distortions due to monetary and fiscal policy. Production and productivity need to be understood independently in order to understand how they work together.

For a short period of time, such as one year, economic output (production) depends upon the number of people who are working and the amount of time they work. For example, if last year an economy employed one million people and if this year the number increases by 30,000, the economic output would increase by 3 percent (with our simplifying assumptions). The same result would be obtained if the original number of people increased their working hours by 3 percent.

Suppose that the number of workers remains constant but the population increases because of births and retirements. The economic output per capita decreases. Here, we need to be mindful of the words we use. Sometimes, this condition would be described as a reduced standard of living, but that would be true only if standard of living were defined as production per capita. Whether or not such a circumstance would improve or reduce the quality of life cannot be known in advance; it depends on the details. In a free society that is functioning well, we should assume the new configuration came about because citizens made choices they believed would indeed improve their lives.

Productivity is a measure of economic output per unit of labor. Imagine a man digging a trench using a shovel of 1900 vintage. He is then given a modern shovel with all the benefits of metallurgical and manufacturing developments. Because the new shovel is essentially unbreakable and possesses a blade that remains sharp, he may be able to dig 50 percent more trench in a day's work, in which case his productivity has increased 50 percent. Such simple examples are rarely possible in our modern economy but the concept remains the same.

Increasing the productivity of workers is one of the building blocks for improving our material standard of living. Without productivity increases, the population and the number of workers could double but the economic output per capita would be the same. On the other hand, the population and number of workers could remain the same and yet produce continuous growth and economic output if there is a continuous growth in productivity. Almost every benefit we enjoy today is directly or indirectly the result of economic growth from increased productivity.

Since the development of the industrial age, population growth and productivity have been linked in a particular way. Some improvements in manufacturing processes and other factors of economic production are only viable if the market for the product is large. That is, there must be many customers to justify the large expenditures necessary to set up mass production, which was a major contributor to the amazing growth and economic prosperity of the twentieth century. Population growth and increasing prosperity allowed the development of ever more productive processes. Another way of describing this idea is that a larger market allows more division of labor through specialization.

Productivity depends upon more than advances in materials and manufacturing processes. The health of a population affects how many people are able to work and how effectively they can do their work. Again, the twentieth century, and particularly the first part of it, brought many improvements to public health. As a simple representative example, life expectancy in the United States went from approximately 47 in 1900 to 77 in 2000.

Productivity may also depend on the education level of the population, but this effect is different in nature than public health. Education will be studied in a later chapter. For this chapter, it is enough to say that the link between general education and productivity is not as strong as commonly believed and in some cases runs in the other direction. That is, general education may be driven by economic growth rather than the other way around.

Division of Labor, Specialization

As a society becomes larger and more wealthy, it can afford the investment necessary to take advantage of the division of labor, which is another way of saying that tasks become more specialized. This is by far the most significant contributor to the huge increases in material standard of living in the twentieth century. In this regard, many people will think of the assembly line for the Ford Model T created in the first years of the twentieth century. But the division of labor was well known and was producing benefits at least 150 years earlier. The rapid growth of population and wealth in the United States allowed a great acceleration of specialization.

When a person or an organization acquires knowledge, skills, and equipment devoted to a specific subject or activity, the result offers two potential benefits. It may be that the particular task is only possible with great specialization, such as heart surgery. Or, the specialization may mean that a particular task can be done more efficiently. Consider the example of a household appliance that might contain more than 1,000 parts produced by dozens if not hundreds of companies located in multiple states and countries. Because each of those parts is produced by firms with special capabilities, it is possible to offer the high-quality appliance to the consumer for a cost many times less than what it would be if a single company tried to produce all of the parts.

At the same time that we are enjoying the benefits from specialization, we are also aware of the associated social impact. We tend to pay more attention to the effect on employment than we do to other outcomes. A useful phrase that captures the essence of the influence on employment is "dispersed gain but focused pain." The first part of the phrase captures the idea that the reduction of costs and the improvement in quality that comes from division of labor are benefits that can be enjoyed by all citizens. The second part acknowledges that sometimes the division of labor has a negative effect on the employment of a very small percentage of the population. A couple of examples will help illustrate this.

Walmart and Amazon are examples of specialization that arise from economies of scale and expertise in management and distribution. Both companies have made shopping easier and less expensive for almost all citizens, thus providing a very broad, incremental benefit to many people. However, natural results of the business model of those companies include the closure of many smaller, local businesses and a downward pressure on the wages of low-skilled workers.

Moving manufacturing and service operations out of the United States to other countries is a form of specialization that has been widely and strongly criticized in recent political contests. Here, it is especially easy to see the "focused pain." When some part of a business is moved offshore, it may result in direct loss of employment for a small number of United States citizens. Those who lost their jobs pay a high price for a small but widespread reduction of cost for all other citizens.

These types of specialization have been going on for a long time. In general, society held that the ongoing achievement of dispersed gain was worth the focused pain. One reason for that assessment was that many of those who were impacted by specialization were able to gain acceptable, if not better, employment elsewhere. Over the past few decades, this has increasingly been less true. As a result, companies who implement these forms of specialization are increasingly criticized for the negative effects. However, a central point of this book is that these companies are responding to the economic votes of citizens.

Demographics and Social Relations

Demographic issues including the aging of our population, birth rates, retirement, funding for Social Security, immigration, and others are already part of our public discussion. Therefore, in this book we only need to discuss a few points that are not a part of the common discussion.

Two points capture the essential understanding needed here. The first is the extent to which our entire social and economic structures have been built upon certain demographic assumptions, some of which are now breaking down. Second, those structures established social relationships among groups, specifically groups defined by age and employment. Because the assumptions are breaking down, we are facing adjustments and compromises that will be settled politically. Therefore, citizens need knowledge of the underlying factors. We will look at two of the most significant issues: retirement and unemployment.

As the number of people in retirement increases, so does the challenge of paying for the retirement. Social Security and Medicare were designed under the assumption that the ratio of the number of people who were employed, and therefore paying payroll taxes, to the number of retired people would remain high enough to sustain the system. For example, in 1950 this ratio was approximately seven while projections for 2030 show a ratio well below three. At the time of this writing, the Social Security Administration has just reached the point where the funds paid out are larger than the taxes taken in. From this point forward, the growing demands on Social Security and Medicare will require increased payroll taxes, reduction of benefits, or additional government debt—or likely a combination of all three. Different groups of citizens will have different views of how this problem should be solved.

Even as originally designed—that is, with a high ratio of workers to retirees—Social Security was not intended to cover nearly all the cost of retirement. Private savings, together with private and public pensions, were required to make up the difference. Many people have inadequate private savings to supplement Social Security benefits. That fact will enter directly into the debate discussed in the above paragraph. Public pensions (associated with government and government-related entities) are significantly underfunded. What that means is that local governments, school systems, and so on, do not have nearly enough funds to pay for the benefits expected by current and future retirees. Citizens will see significant political pressure to raise taxes to fully fund the promises of these pensions. While the problem is not as large, many company pension funds are also underfunded. There will be political pressure to have taxpayers provide the additional funding. The issues of pension funding, both public and private, will pit the interests of one group of citizens against other groups.

The second significant issue is unemployment and underemployment, both of which underlie the much-discussed subject of economic inequality. Inequality and associated subjects are now major points of contention in political debates. A later chapter is devoted to inequality. In this chapter, the relevant point is that proposals for increased taxes and government redistribution programs will also pit the interests of one group against another—and, as we will see later, not address the underlying causes.

SOCIAL STRUCTURE

"Civilized societies have built up a vast set of cultural imperatives and conventions governing people's interactions with one another and the state. Very few are written down, and most of us are not fully aware of the extent to which societal forces, religion, and education direct even the minutest of our choices day by day."
Alan Greenspan

"There is no school equal to a decent home and no teacher equal to a virtuous parent."
Gandhi

Within the meaning of "social structure," I include institutions, relationships, and those aspects of worldview that most directly affect how a society configures itself and how it functions. Our social structure has changed a great deal since World War II. The new world order that emerged following World War II went beyond the obvious geopolitical and economic changes. A new psychological and spiritual order was arising also. While this new order brought benefits, we can now see it also brought about changes that have damaged our social structure—in some cases, to the point of breakdown.

At the time of this writing, the damaged social structures along with related problems dominate public discussion. However, before describing some of our troubles, I want to be clear that a great deal of what is good and strong in our society remains; it is built into our social structure. But for our time, it is essential to understand what has gone wrong, why it went wrong, how it changed our social structure, and what the consequences of those changes are.

Our description will begin by simply listing a few of the obvious problems, things that are frequently observed and discussed. These are issues the vast majority of Americans recognize and agree on. Many young people reach age 18 woefully underprepared for life—in their character, in basic schooling, and increasingly in mental and physical health. Many Americans have inadequate access to healthcare. A stable nuclear family is far from the norm. A growing number of children are in households with single parents who are often under economic pressure. The use of drugs and other behaviors that misguidedly aim to moderate physical, social, and emotional pain are now common headline news. Incarceration rates have approximately tripled since 1970. Economic and social inequality are great enough to cause social breakdown if they are not addressed. Social and political division and conflict are at historical levels, causing many problems, not least of which is the inability to find solutions. The levels of trust among citizens and between citizens and institutions are at all-time lows. Respect for authority is low and declining. Society is sorting itself to such a degree that one group cannot begin to appreciate what another group experiences. The list could go on but is sufficient for now.

These problems in our society are of course symptoms of underlying social structures that have failed to work properly. Social structures are built upon our worldview, which contains what we value. Furthermore, these problems (symptoms) did not suddenly appear;

they have been forming and building for many decades. Some of what we can now see retrospectively as early symptoms were not recognized as problems. As time passed and as some symptoms were seen as small problems, they were treated as such. That is, the treatment was to apply some patch or mask such that the symptom appeared to go away. This can be compared to recognizing that we have a small health problem or that a bridge has small cracks beginning to form at crucial spots. We take action to make what we observe go away, or at least to be hidden. These temporary fixes can only work for a while. At some point, it becomes clear that we have a serious health problem or that the bridge may come crashing down.

As a society, we are in a period of transition because our problems are increasing in number and intensity. In recent decades, the old patches and fixes have been attempted again and again but are no longer sufficient to hide the symptoms. Often, those attempts to patch seem only to make problems worse. At the same time, no viable solutions are in view. I used the word "transition" to describe our time because some people still believe that the symptoms are the real problem and that there is no fundamental structural issue. In this view, we simply need to find a new treatment for the symptoms. Fortunately, a growing number of people believe, or at least suspect, that our problems are foundational and that therefore we may face difficult and expensive work to find real solutions. If our analogy is health, we need expensive medication or surgery. If our analogy is a bridge, disruptive and expensive repairs are needed.

During this time of transition, we are experiencing increased social stress, anxiety, fear, and conflict. These emotional states are strong enough that many people believe it is our conflict and divisiveness that is the fundamental problem, but that is not true. Our social stress and conflict are the result of two factors. First, we are facing problems that have proved unsolvable to this point. Second, groups within society hold diverging worldviews. Both factors must be better understood if we are to find a productive way forward. If we understand the underlying, foundational issues, perhaps we can moderate the emotional climate sufficiently so that we can work toward real solutions.

Such an understanding requires an investigation into why these problems developed, why the structures changed, and why the process went on for so long without correction. Only by doing this hard work of grasping what really happened and why it happened can we hope to see a way forward.

While the 1950s are sometimes regarded as golden years, in retrospect, we see they really were not. It was simply a time without obvious symptoms. Each subsequent decade revealed more symptoms. Therefore, we need to address a critical question: why did we start going off-track in our social structure? In the 1950s, few people, if any, imagined that 70 years later we would be facing the problems we now have.

The "why" question to be addressed is conceptual, almost philosophical. It is not the question of how we managed to get by with temporary fixes for so long. We will take up that question later. The "why" question can be clarified somewhat by comparing the development of the economic and social structures over the same seventy-year period. As the economic structure developed, it produced the objective benefit of an improved material standard of living, not only for citizens of the United States, but for the majority of people around the world as well. While the economic structure has problems that need to be addressed, what it delivered has been the goal of people through all of history: a better material standard of living.

The same cannot be said for the development of the social structure. No standards from history suggest that it is good for a society for families to break down, for inequality to increase, for trust to decline, for authority and hierarchy to be rejected, for the development of character and virtue to be minimized, and for one group of citizens to force their will upon another. On the contrary, such breakdowns often preceded upheaval in a society, or even the decline of a society. Why then, when early evidence of these trends became visible in our time, did society as a whole behave as if they were good, or at least not bad?

Because the development of social structure is based on worldview, we must begin our search for answers by looking at how our worldview was changing. Two of the most significant influences contributing to changes in worldview are changes in beliefs and environment, the latter often coming about, or at any rate being understood, through new events. An understanding of changes in those two areas will help a great deal in understanding why those social trends began and continued.

For most of 2,000 years, Christianity was the dominant belief system in Western civilization. It was a constant shaper of worldview. It provided commonality of values, ways to understand the world, and the rules about what should and should not be done. It provided a basis for community. It provided both a basis as well as institutions for the training of individuals. All of these things are crucial for a society.

Over the past 150 years, however, Christianity's influence has steadily diminished. The path for this decline was different for the United States than other Western countries. In fact, at times it appeared that Christianity's influence was increasing in the United States while noticeably declining elsewhere. For example, in the 1950s, participation in religion remained strong, even increasing somewhat as a percentage of the population. However, in the following decades, the meanings of *Christian* and *Christianity* started to change. This change was driven by two things. First, ideas in theology and philosophy which had come about in the first part of the twentieth century exerted a powerful influence. Second, the changing social environment began to have as much influence on the meaning of Christianity as Christianity once exerted on the social environment.

Nonetheless, few people in the 1950s would have predicted that by the turn of the millennium the view of many toward Christianity would go from positive to neutral, and that within another decade, the view of many would go from neutral to negative—or simply indifferent. The social significance of this decline is that it no longer provided the social functions and commonality that had been so important for the preceding 2,000 years.

Furthermore, as Christianity declined, it was not replaced by any coherent belief system. What replaced it came from thinking that had its origins in the early part of the century and continued to gain acceptance. A diverse mix of ideas and philosophies circulated, first among the intellectual community and then slowly in general society. But these ideas and beliefs were fragmented and did not stem from common foundations. In fact, the ideas and beliefs were often directly in conflict.

In retrospect, however, two major premises underlie much of the thinking that attempted to replace what Christianity once provided. First, there is no such thing as objective reality or truth. Reality and truth are human constructs. Second, the desires of an individual are paramount. Complete self-autonomy is the highest value.

We now turn to environment. Events of the first half of the twentieth century positioned the United States for a truly new era. Those events were covered in the first part of the book and won't be reviewed here. Instead, we return to an idea also previously mentioned: the hierarchy of human motivations, for which I referenced the Maslow model.

For the first time in history, an entire society was going to experience decades of peace and growing prosperity, conditions necessary for lower levels of the Maslow hierarchy to be more easily satisfied, which in turn would free time and resources to pursue the upper levels. It is in these upper levels where self-esteem, self-actualization, and transcendence are pursued. However, the *ends* and the *means* in the upper levels, are more numerous, ambiguous, and difficult to determine than they are for the lower levels. That is, the objectives of food, shelter, and security are more concrete and immediate than the potential objectives in the upper levels. Furthermore, when pursuing food, shelter, and safety, there are fewer moral considerations. There is little moral decision to be made about whether or not to eat or be safe. What moral decisions exist have to do with the chosen *means*. For example, it is moral to work for food and immoral to steal food.

The situation is different when acting in the upper levels of the Maslow hierarchy, where consideration of morals, virtues, and the common good are relevant to the selection of most ends and means. This brings us to the crux of this consideration. What happens when a society, en masse, begins paying attention to the upper levels of Maslow at the same time that its traditional worldview—the worldview that provided guidance on *should*—is beginning to fracture? More specifically for the United States, what happens when that fracturing results in diverging worldviews, when some people believe that aspects of the traditional worldview are wrong or damaging?

Such was the environment heading into the last half of the twentieth century. In the first half, major world events resulted in the aforementioned new world order that worked together with new ideas in economics, philosophy, religion, and politics to form the backdrop against which big changes would occur in the following 70 years. But in 1950, this backdrop was latent. Only in the following decades, as people were exploring the upper Maslow levels and responding to the changes in worldview, did the results become visible.

Remember, we are pursuing the question of why society did not recognize the potential harm from the many changes that took place in the first half of the century. It is not as if no one saw the changes and understood their potential significance; a number of thinkers made such observations. A fair assessment requires recognizing that new ideas, new processes, new technology, and so on, often take decades for their effects to be obvious. But that fact, while true, does little to illuminate our question. I suggest that a single word, "newness," can help us understand.

This newness includes things which have been addressed earlier in the book, such as the new world order, new economic modes, new perspectives on government, and new technology. It includes things that will be talked about in the chapters ahead such as the structure of money and finance, the path of democracy, and the way all of these things played out in specific applications. Another aspect of newness goes beyond the changes themselves: the pace of change that has sharply accelerated from 1950 until the present. Never in history has a society been required to process so much change in so many domains in so little time.

Here, we will look at an aspect of newness that is more subtle and that was influential in 1950, even if not realized. Considering all of the newness referenced above, it was easier for people to doubt, to think that perhaps things really were different, perhaps the old rules did not apply as much, and maybe some of the principles no longer applied as they did in the past.

Furthermore, as the years passed and trends and circumstances developed that in times past would have provoked caution, society did not experience the consequences predicted by some of the early thinkers who understood what was happening under the surface.

This lack of obvious consequences made it easier to discount earlier insights. It also added weight to the idea that "we are in a different time." Of course, we can now see clearly that consequences were forming but were not easy to perceive because the feedback that would have come from consequences was distorted and moderated. A central theme of this book is to help understand the problems of feedback, of seeing it and responding to it.

A brief summary. At the middle of the last century the United States was poised for unprecedented peace and prosperity. This represented a completely new social situation. The philosophical and circumstantial milieu, together with the sheer newness of so many things, partially explains why ideas and behaviors that in previous times would have raised mitigating forces were either ignored or accepted. What we have not yet addressed is why individual citizens made the choices they did. Could not our society just as easily have taken paths that would have avoided the list of problems with which we opened this chapter? Put another way, why in the pursuit of satisfying the upper levels of the motivational hierarchy did citizens make the choices that led to our present challenges?

We can find the foundation for the answers by returning to the fundamental principles covered in the first part of the book. Physical nature and human nature result in a world in which an ordered society, a society that is peaceful and prosperous, is not natural. The peace and prosperity we enjoy is the result of historically special conditions but not so special that we can avoid constraints that have always existed for any society. Whatever degree of order, peace, and prosperity a society manages to develop must be carefully maintained, or what was built over much time will disappear in little time.

As we've seen in earlier chapters, consequences of actions help individuals, and therefore societies, adjust behavior before too much damage is done. Whether a society is simple or complex, small or large, poor or prosperous, it is guided in its development and maintenance by the consequences of actions. However, if for whatever reason, people cannot see and understand what is happening, or if they choose to ignore it, they will not respond in ways that bring about correction.

For the United States, beginning in the middle of the twentieth century, the feedback process was altered by historically unique events. Consequences were more difficult to see and recognize. Others were seen but could be patched over and needed action postponed. Those special geopolitical, economic, and demographic events have been noted several times in earlier chapters. At this point, however, those events have largely played out. Thus, the consequences of decisions and actions from the last 70 years—consequences which up to this point have been mitigated by those unique events—must now be properly dealt with in our generation.

As noted earlier in the chapter, our society is in transition; we are coming to terms with what has happened. Long-standing expectations are not being met, and previous means of patching and postponing are not working. As a society, we are in the process of understanding and accepting what has happened. But whether a specific person understands and accepts or not, the consequences are being felt. Thus, citizens can feel uneasy, concerned, anxious, and afraid without yet grasping the full picture of what is going on.

What I've said so far in this chapter helps us understand our situation at the beginning of the twenty-first century. However, it is not adequate to explain our situation in the early years of the 2020s (the time of this writing). Something new has occurred, something that led to behavior today that would have been hard to believe only 20 years before. Who would have imagined the following examples: some cities defunded police departments and effectively decriminalized "small" thefts; a proclaimed socialist became a serious presidential candidate; some public schools contributed to gender confusion in children; a violent event associated with a presidential inauguration unfolded at the capitol; mere pronoun usage generated anger; elected officials supported a monetary theory that said government debt can be increased without consequences.

Sometimes, when big events happen suddenly, we assume the reasons for the event are also recent, but that is not usually the case. More often, conditions have been forming for a long time but don't produce the big event until a tipping point is reached or a catalyst triggers it.

I suggest that the catalyst was the 2008 financial crisis, not because of the economic pain but because of what it revealed about social and economic structures. It became clear that long-standing expectations were unlikely to be met and that this was true for multiple areas, including economic progress, economic equality, equality of opportunity, education, healthcare, and retirement. Concerns grew in the years following 2008 because no solutions were in view. These problems had two effects upon citizens. First, there was the objective impact on measures of well-being. Second, and more importantly, there was the emotional impact of unmet expectations together with the realization that future expectations were also unlikely to be met.

Because it is in human nature, when we feel injured and disappointed, we are likely to look for circumstances or a group to blame. A specific example particularly relevant to this chapter is the blame directed at the elite class. The development of an elite class is normal within society, even within a democracy. The problem arises from the implicit bargain discussed in the earlier chapter, "Thinking Like A Ruler." Recall that in this implicit bargain the populace yielded a great deal of ongoing power to a ruling group that in turn was to manage all of social life, most importantly economics, for the good of everyone. As the failures of this bargain were clearly revealed in the 2008 crisis, a negative reaction to the elites grew rapidly.

The negative reaction was fueled by more than simply an objective failure of the bargain. The "elites," which include more than just those in government, had for some time been separating from much of the populace. By the 2008 presidential election, this separation had progressed such that some elites openly disparaged portions of the populace. In return, some of the populace looked with scorn at the elites. Over the following eight years this separation continued to grow, reaching a tipping point in the 2016 presidential election in which Donald Trump, explicitly cast as anti-elite, defeated Hillary Clinton, cast as the epitome of the elite class.

The election was both a response to what had happened and a catalyst for what was about to happen. Political and social divisiveness, each of which had been building for years, accelerated rapidly. A new emotional environment formed, one in which polarization and divisiveness affected more than political and social debates. It extended to the family dinner table, to marriages, and to groups which only a few years earlier seemed joined in solidarity. This hardening of positions, this willingness to weaken or break long-standing relationships, was new in its severity.

However, that was just the beginning. The presidential election also catalyzed other behavior that was either new or newly extreme. Tolerance and free speech have suffered greatly, creating a movement that has its own name: "cancel culture." Some cities reduced the funding or scope of activities for police in support of a movement that bore the slogan, "defund the police." (And as would be expected given human nature, those cities experienced an increase in crime.) Differing standards of justice are in open view such that activities praised in one group are declared antisocial or illegal in another. Science, which was perhaps the last of the respected sources of authority, lost much of its standing because it became openly politicized. This partial list of social changes and movements is offered simply as evidence that a new emotional climate has developed.

The 2020 presidential election confirmed that these behaviors were not the transitory result of a particular person in the office of president. All of the example behaviors listed above continued after the election.

Any society, certainly any free society, is always dealing with objective issues in the realms of economics, freedom, equality, rights, and responsibilities. If the society has the necessary degree of solidarity coming from shared values and common goals, the issues may be vigorously debated, but the debate and struggle comes from within. That is, the vast majority of citizens see themselves as part of a coherent society and are working from within to improve it. In such a social milieu, the debates and solutions proceed with an appropriate mix of rational arguments and emotional energy. However, if a normal—we could say stable—milieu does not exist, the debate will turn largely emotional and will not produce real solutions.

I believe that our current social milieu is not normal and that we therefore need something additional to understand our circumstances. We need a word that can capture a social-emotional state that has been characterized as fearful, anxious, angry, confrontational, polarized, regressed, alienated, irresponsible, intolerant, coercive, and disordered. When introducing a new element, a new word, into an emotionally charged conversation, the choice of the word is important. Often, common words that come to mind will have multiple connotations that will be negative for some and positive for others. Using such a word requires constant clarification and carries the constant risk of misunderstanding. Therefore, I have elected to use *anomie*, a word used by Emile Durkheim in the late nineteenth century to represent the disintegration and disordering that was taking place in Europe as it faced economic and social changes at the same time it was abandoning Christianity.

What causes a state of anomie to develop within a society, and what the response of individuals will be, depend upon the particular details of that society. However, the categories are generally the same: economic and social stress, rapid change, and the loss of social norms and guidance. Likewise, the responses of individuals are particular but tend to create results in these categories: solidarity is weakened, traditional morals and virtues are no longer seen as valid or constraining, traditional sources of authority are rejected, personal responsibility is minimized, individualism increases, individuals "check out" of society at an increasing rate.

Previous and upcoming chapters discuss particular events and circumstances that contributed to the development of anomie. Many of these are of the same type Europe experienced in the late nineteenth century. In this chapter, I want to emphasize a new element that arises from the opportunity for an entire society to pursue the upper levels of Maslow's hierarchy. After seventy years of experience with that opportunity, we see that it did not turn out well for many people who pursued power, wealth, sex, absolute autonomy, and entertainment. Furthermore, even if some individuals feel they obtained a level of satisfaction through those pursuits, the consequences for the broader society were often negative.

Anomie will affect society long before the majority of citizens manifest the extreme characteristics noted above. A society may be paralyzed or hijacked if only a small percentage of people exhibit the extreme characteristics. All that is required is the majority to either not know how to respond, or choose not to respond, to the anomie-driven behavior of the minority.

Two points are crucial for this chapter. First, we have this new dimension to deal with: the state of anomie exists and is intensifying.

Second, as long as anomie has a controlling influence, society will be unable to find solutions and a way forward. This inability comes about because people acting out of anomie tend to hold to their understanding and actions regardless of knowledge, insight, and evidence. Furthermore, those acting out of anomie tend to see the only solution as coercing others to conform to their beliefs and actions.

Thus, anomie directly impacts a central theme of this book, which is that for many decades we did not see, understand, or fundamentally address social feedback, and what we did see and act on, we did so with mitigation and procrastination. The critical underlying assumption is that we have the potential to see and understand, and when we do so, we have the ability to debate and find a solution. However, in a state of anomie, the willingness—and perhaps even the ability—to see and accept reality and to engage in democratic debate is greatly weakened. As such, what role will the principles, understanding, and applications presented in this book have?

The answer is that, in the end, reality always wins. Actions have consequences that can only be ignored for a period of time. Second, as with everything involving humans, there is a spectrum. Some of our citizens are completely caught up in anomie but others are not at all. For this second group, a proper understanding will help slow the spread of anomie and eventually contribute toward real solutions.

We can return now to the explanation of how we arrived in our current condition. First, a recap. Structural problems that had been developing for decades were recognized by a growing number of observers as one millennium ended and a new one began. But it was the 2008 financial crisis that precipitated the widespread realization that many things were not working and many expectations were not going to be met. I suggest the financial crisis, and several years following it, was a crucial junction. At that point, we had two paths we could follow. One was to continue with the same understanding and methods of mitigating and postponing. The other path was to accept that our previous understanding and methods had in fact caused many of the newly recognized problems, and therefore, it was time to regain an understanding of what had really happened and what was required to get back on a better track.

The second path would have been a difficult choice for many reasons. Even if as a society we would have had the will at that time to take on the hard tasks, I think we may not have had the preparation necessary to reach a new understanding. Whatever the reasons, the first path was chosen. Of course, this choice between two paths was not explicit. There was no vote. There was scarcely any public debate. The choice was simply made.

Continuing to follow the first path has further confirmed that it is not working well for most citizens. In fact, inequality in a broad sense, not only wealth and income, accelerated in the years following 2008. Thus began the process described above that brought us to a developing state of anomie in which some groups are not looking for solutions but are looking to destroy existing structures, erase and rewrite American history, and in a few extreme cases, to destroy what we know as the nuclear family.

Our social structure is an integral part of our governance; therefore, some of the ideas in this chapter will show up in the upcoming chapter called "Rulership Structure."

MONETARY AND FINANCIAL STRUCTURE

> *"Let me issue and control a nation's money and I care not who writes the laws."*
> Mayer Amschel Rothschild

Our monetary and financial structure is the least understood of the structures that bring about social change, yet it is also by far the most powerful. It is the least understood for three reasons. Because money brings power and appears to bring wealth, human nature constantly drives some individuals to interfere in the natural development and function of money. Second, any such interference brings about consequences difficult to foresee and understand. Third, under modern governments, such interference has resulted in incredibly complex monetary and financial instruments and mechanisms. The tremendous power the monetary and financial structure enables for the purpose of shaping society comes about because the modern form of monetary interference concentrates economic power in just a few small groups. We will look at how this situation developed and how it impacts society today.

From this point forward, unless specifically necessary, I will refer simply to monetary structure to include both it and the financial structure. This can be done without confusion because almost all of the complexity and damaging power of the financial structure derive directly from our monetary structure.

Today, we live under a monetary structure that is totally new in all of history. That structure is all that any of us have experienced. Therefore, for us to understand its impact upon social and economic structures, we need a reference point and an appreciation of how our current structure developed. While understanding the development process is not simple, I believe it is essential to have a general grasp of what happened; without such understanding, I think we cannot grasp how our current monetary structure was able to drastically alter our social and economic structures.

For the reference point, I will describe a society, the gold society, that uses gold as their money and that has no government interaction with the money. Such societies have existed historically, though rarely, in the past several hundred years.

For the development process, I will give historical examples that illuminate some of the motivations and mechanisms on the road that eventually led to our current system. Finally, using the background of the previous two steps, I will describe some of the important characteristics of our monetary structure that give it unprecedented power to alter our society in so many ways.

We begin our investigation of the gold society by establishing a crucial fact; the society uses gold because of a preceding, lengthy process. For our purposes, we only need capture a few facts about that development. Money did not come into being because a government created it. Rather, money developed in a slow process as people needed a better way than direct barter to exchange goods and services. In that development process, societies have used an interesting array of things as money, including salt, shells, animal skins, and cattle, just to name a few. The common characteristic is that money was something physical, relatively scarce, had some non-money value in society, and took effort to procure. As the result of this long process, and as the level of exchange in the world grew, societies gravitated toward metals as their money, finally settling on gold and silver as dominant. In this final state, more money could enter society only if some people invested effort to mine and refine gold or silver.

In the gold society, the monetary structure is so simple that it can be ignored. This is true because it came about naturally. Gold was simply one of the things produced by the society. In addition to using gold as adornment, its intrinsic value, it was also used as a means of exchange. If one person wanted to acquire a cow, they didn't have to gather up multiple other items to exchange with the owner to purchase the animal. Instead, over time the society naturally established that a cow was worth a certain weight of gold. And because in the gold society government has no role in producing or controlling money, the monetary structure has no explicit effect on the economic or social structure. It can be said to be neutral in that regard.

This concept of a monetary structure being neutral with regard to social change does not mean everyone will earn the same or will acquire the same amount of wealth. As we saw in the first part of the book, those types of differences must occur in a free society. Neutrality means that the monetary structure can't be manipulated by one group to the detriment of other groups.

What happens in the gold society if a person wants to borrow money? They must find another person or group of people who, through the act of saving, have accumulated more gold than they need for their immediate use. The two parties agree upon the terms of the loan, which of course includes the interest rate. If for whatever reason those who have saved gold are inclined to hold it rather than make a loan, the person will either not be able to obtain it or pay a much higher interest rate.

We now turn from our reference society and look at a few historical developments that will help us comprehend how our modern system came about.

Human nature made the most important of these developments inevitable. Because of the unique and essential nature of money, those in power, specifically those in rulership power, have for thousands of years attempted to manipulate the monetary structure to increase their power. As a ruler became more powerful, he would gain exclusive control of money. Rulers almost always wanted to spend more than they could acquire by taxes or conquest. A common mechanism was to cheapen the money by replacing some of the gold by a cheaper metal. For example, if a citizen paid taxes with 10 units of gold, the ruler could melt that gold and mix in a cheaper metal, producing 11 coins. When citizens caught on to what happened—and they always did—the ruler would pass laws forcing citizens to pay taxes in the most valuable (that is, the older) coins. The effect of this mechanism was, of course, to shift wealth from citizens to the rulership.

The mechanism of cheapening coins has practical and political limitations. The larger the percentage of cheaper metal, the more obvious is the substitution. If the process moves along too quickly, the prices of goods will increase quickly, which in turn will bring about unproductive citizen activity or more extreme, different forms of rebellion. Thus, rulers were always looking for new ways to cheapen—to inflate—the money supply without producing negative reactions from citizens.

Because the money was still physical, still containing a fraction of gold, it was easy for citizens to see what was happening. They could also see and understand something that is more difficult to see today. Citizens who operated physically and economically furthest from the center of rulership suffered the most. The new, cheaper coins would first be spent by the rulers, then by those physically and economically closest to the rulers. Those who had the opportunity to use the cheaper coins first were able to buy goods and services at the old prices before they rose. However, those who were far removed received the new coins later. Thus, it was more likely that those citizens were using the older, more valuable coins to purchase goods and services whose prices had already increased.

The next big development step began several hundred years ago in the early part of modernity. First, as nation-states developed and economies grew, the rulership group rapidly increased its power. However, these groups still struggled with how to spend more than they could tax, borrow, or take from other countries. The solution, which took a couple of centuries to work through, was the establishment of government-controlled banking. While this took various forms in different countries and times, the essence was the same. Government granted monopoly powers to banks with regard to money. Banks, in turn, would use this power to help finance government.

Particularly in the United States, this was a messy process beginning almost immediately following independence. Banks were trying to maximize profit. The primary way they did so was to loan more money than savers had deposited with them. With our gold society in view, it might seem this behavior by banks would be illegal because they were loaning "money" they simply conjured. However, the government offered protection by declaring that such behavior was not illegal. Instead, the average citizen saver had to monitor the banks. If depositors began suspecting their bank had loaned more money than they should, they would start demanding their deposits back from the bank. This was the classic "bank run." Because the bank had loaned more money than it had, it could not repay the depositors. In extreme cases, the bank would default, resulting in the owners losing their money and the depositors losing some of their money.

As these bank runs and panics became more severe, both the banks and the government needed a solution. The chosen solution had two parts. The first was to create the Federal Reserve in 1913. The second was to create the Federal Deposit Insurance Corporation (FDIC) in 1933. Banks needed protection, and the government needed banks. As these institutions matured, the net effect was that the government, working through those institutions, could effectively create money on demand to bail out a bank in trouble. The solution was effective in almost totally eliminating bank runs. However, the long-term significance of the solution was not its success regarding bank runs but rather that it was built on ideas and legislation that would eventually result in our current monetary structure.

The next step in the development process is not as easy to present in concrete terms. Instead, it will be explained using key events. Following World War II, with most of the world in disarray, the major countries agreed on a monetary system in which the dominant money—what was called the reserve currency—would be the dollar. The agreement provided that a foreign country could sell dollars to the United States in exchange for gold. That is, there was a loose connection between the reserve currency (the dollar) and gold. However, this was true only for foreign governments. Ordinary citizens could not redeem currency for gold.

This agreement, called the Bretton Woods Agreement, was open to abuse by the United States because the government could issue more dollars than it could honestly back up with gold. That is what happened. Primarily because of the costs of the Vietnam War and of social programs implemented in the 1960s, the United States created a flood of dollars. By 1970, other countries recognized this inflation of the money supply and began submitting large quantities of dollars to the United States, demanding gold per the Bretton Woods Agreement. Because the United States could no longer honor the agreement, President Nixon effectively abolished it in 1971. The United States would no longer exchange gold for dollars.

For the first time in history, there was no anchor for money. That is, the supply of money was not limited by the production of gold or by any physical effort. The new arrangement was called a *fiat* monetary system because money could now be created by decree. Few people at the time understood what this meant for the future. It was the culmination of a long process in which a monumental shift occurred in the foundation for money. For most of human history, money represented something tangible, something that required effort to produce, something that had value in its own right, above and beyond its role as a means of exchange. When all pretense of anchoring money to gold (something tangible and requiring effort to produce) was eliminated, money became nothing more than debt.

The 1970s were a period of turmoil and confusion under this monetary system—which could scarcely be called a system at all because each country had to figure out what they would do with their own currency. It was also a period of price inflation. By 1980, the consumer price inflation rate was over 13 percent. At the same time, economic growth was minimal. Those years thus earned the moniker "stagflation." When President Reagan was elected, he mandated that the Federal Reserve get inflation under control. As with all corrections, it was a painful time for the country. Some interest rates reached higher than 15 percent. However, within a couple of years of his election, economic growth resumed.

(Refer to the Economics chapter in the fundamentals part of the book, and to the Economic Structure chapter earlier in this part for more background on concepts such as growth and inflation. In what follows, I am reporting the official numbers.)

As a result of that painful experience, the United States government, including the Federal Reserve, were vigilant about price inflation. Arguably, the control of inflation became the number-one goal of monetary policy. In fact, for thirty years following 1990 the consumer price index (CPI) averaged about 2.3 percent. And economic growth continued until the 2008 crisis.

As a society, we have a tendency to think "this time is different" or "we are in a new era." So, having a number of years of moderate inflation together with economic growth led to the idea of "a new economy." Furthermore, as government liabilities, both formal debt and social obligations, grew ever larger and yet seemingly did not affect consumer prices or growth, some economists and politicians proposed that government deficit spending and increasing government debt no longer mattered as they did in the past. This eventually led to "modern monetary theory," which attempted to provide justification for largely ignoring spending and debt.

A constant focus in this book is that fundamental principles always apply, no matter how new or different things may temporarily appear. The crisis of 2008 revealed that the "new economy" was not new. Furthermore, at this point in the book, we can understand that "modern monetary theory" represents nothing more than what rulership has always attempted: finding ways to cheapen money while minimizing negative reactions from citizens. For two years prior to the time of this writing, inflation has been at forty-year highs. This should demonstrate the error of "modern thinking" about money.

That concludes our sketch of how we ended up with our current monetary structure, a structure that perfects the cheapening of money. It is perfect in this regard because (1) no effort is required to create more money, and (2) its mechanisms and harm are difficult for the average citizen to discern, which in turn means minimal negative feedback from the citizenry. We will now examine how our monetary structure alters the economic and social structures.

The power to alter other structures is derived largely from the centralized monetary authority of the federal government. No other entity can create or regulate money unless, of course, the federal government authorizes it to do so. This means that the federal government can run deficits and borrow money in ways no other government or entity can. In turn, that allows the federal government to exercise a lot of control over state and local governments as well as other entities, such as businesses, though the control of the latter is often more indirect.

Today, newly created money enters the economy through two primary mechanisms. For decades, the primary mechanism was the banking system, which, following government policy, would increase or decrease the volume of loans made. This path resulted in money flowing into what is sometimes called the "real economy." The second mechanism, which has become much more important in the past couple of decades, and especially since the 2008 crisis, is through direct government spending. Both paths, however, have the same underlying foundation: the increase of debt. Through the banking system, the debt is incurred by businesses and individuals. Through government spending, the debt is incurred by the federal government. Because both share a common foundation of borrowing—and because borrowing is the monetary means by which social and economic structures are altered—we need a proper understanding of what borrowing truly represents.

Let's return to our reference point, the gold society, and expand on our previous comments about borrowing. The person who has gold to lend has obtained it by consuming less than he has produced. That is, he has saved. For example, if in a given year he produced goods that he sold for ten units of gold, but he only spent eight units to purchase goods for consumption, his savings were increased by two units of gold. He has postponed consumption until some later time. The other person, the borrower, needs to consume more this year than he will produce. Perhaps he is starting a business or maybe some personal misfortune has resulted in extra expenses. The borrower goes to the lender and makes a deal for a loan. The essence of this arrangement is that the lender has handed over his "saved consumption" so that the borrower may use it. Of course, the expectation is that at some later time the lender will return that saved consumption plus some amount for interest.

During the term of the loan, the lender does not have access to the saved consumption. If something happens in his life such that he needs to consume more than he can produce, plus more than whatever he has retained in savings, he will have to resort to borrowing by approaching another lender (saver). Here is the crucial point: what is borrowed in a loan arrangement are real resources—it is previous production that has not been consumed.

In today's monetary structure, this linkage between saver and borrower has steadily weakened to the point that it is almost broken. Stated differently, today a great deal of debt is incurred without any involvement of savers. Much of what we now call borrowing is something different from what has been understood from all of human history up until very recent times. It takes place not by using saved resources but rather by the creation of money. And that makes a great deal of difference to the social and economic structures.

Now, let us look at borrowing under today's structure. Current regulations allow the banking system to create nine dollars of money for one dollar deposited into a checking account. In today's financial structure, this process happens through multiple banks. For simplicity, I will talk as if the entire process takes place within one bank.

The interested reader can look up "fractional reserve banking" for a more detailed explanation.

Our scenario begins with a person depositing $1,000 into their checking account. On the same day, another person wants to borrow $9,000. Because this is within the limit of the law, the banker can loan $9,000 even though no one has actually saved that money. Compare this to the borrowing example above in the gold society. First, note that the $1,000 deposit is not savings; it went into a checking account. The depositor can immediately spend that money to buy groceries or anything else they want. In this case, $9,000 of purchasing power—that is, money—was created out of thin air. There is no linkage whatsoever between saving and borrowing.

With these two borrowing scenarios, one from the gold society and one from today, we can look at the differences between the two and begin to appreciate the impact upon society. I want to again emphasize that the following examples are real in the effects they illustrate but are simplified. Furthermore, exactly what implications result, as well as the timing, depend upon particular circumstances.

The first thing most people will see is that the money in circulation, that is, the potential purchasing power of the society, did not change in the reference scenario, whereas it increased by $9,000 in the example based on today's structure. What would happen if many people within a community borrowed money? A lot of new money would be circulating in the community, but the production of goods and services within the community would not have increased. As a result, the tendency would be for prices to rise—what we call price inflation. The borrowers see an advantage because they borrowed for the purpose of immediate spending. Thus, they acquire goods and services at the existing prices, whereas others in the community will be making purchases later in time, after prices have begun to rise.

Continuing with the above story, who in the community are likely to suffer the most loss? One group will be those who are dependent upon savings or a fixed income. People in that group must pay higher prices for what they need and do so using the same savings and income they had before price inflation began. Thus, economic inequality will develop between those who first receive and spend the new money, along with those whose income tends to increase with increasing prices, and those for whom the opposites are true.

The next observation may not be quite so obvious. In the gold society, both parties must be willing participants in the borrowing process. If there are no people who want to borrow and if there are no savers who want to lend, loans don't happen. While there is no principle that says it must be true, general experience shows there are always people who want to borrow. The limiting factor is usually the availability of savings at attractive terms. Thus, in the gold society, both savers and borrowers have some control over the economic structure. Let's look at a simple example to illustrate.

Again, we begin our example with the gold society. A group of people want to borrow money to fund a new business venture, and they begin looking for a group of savers. However, many in the community, including many of those with surplus savings to loan, are concerned that the new venture is not good for the community as a whole. Perhaps it will increase unemployment or will increase pollution. It could be any number of reasons. In any event, there are not enough savers who are willing to lend money for this new venture. Of course, the opposite case could be true. The general sentiment, including those of the savers, might be very favorable, in which case plenty of funds would be made available at attractive terms. In either case, multiple parties within the community have contributed to what the economic structure will look like.

What does this example look like under today's monetary structure? The biggest difference is that the group of people who are savers have no role to play in the decision. The banking system takes the place of the saving group. But the source of funding, and therefore the motivation, of the banks is different than those of the savers in the gold society. The banking system is not dependent upon lending saved resources. It can create money to lend based on only a small fraction of checking account deposits. Because what is being loaned out are not real resources, and not the result of previous thrift, the banking system is motivated simply by making money on loans. While perhaps individuals in the banking business may care about the long-term economic structure, the banking system as a whole need have no concern. Therefore, the driving force for changes in the economic structure are much different than in the gold society.

Here, we see a subtle yet important way in which the economic "voting" of citizens has been weakened. In the lender-borrower relationship, the group of citizens who would normally be voting on the "lender" side of the deal have been moved out of the picture. To illustrate this, we will pick up the example from just above in which a loan was being considered in the gold society. We will see how that could play out under today's monetary structure. Let's assume that the loan was denied in the gold society because many people, including most of the savers, thought that the new venture would hurt employment opportunities in the community. And, if it hurt employment opportunities, it would likely have negative social effects also.

Under today's system, however, the savers have no vote; it is up to the bank. As already noted, the bank can create 90 percent of the money required for the loan. The primary concern to the bank will be whether or not the new venture will be able to repay the loan plus interest, thus providing a profit to the bank. While the bank is not obligated to worry about the employment picture for the community, it *may* consider that factor in their decision. Whether the bank does so or not, and if it does so, whether it was correct or not in its assessments, is a secondary point. The key understanding with regard to the economic voting of citizens is that a single entity, the bank, cast the entire lender-side vote. Thus, the bank and the borrowers control this particular factor that helps determine the economic structure.

Because the next several observations deal specifically with the financial structure, we will describe the structure by listing some of the more common institutions. Banks, of course, are part of the financial structure but are unique because only they can truly create money. All other parts of the financial structure must rely ultimately on the banking system. The financial structure includes brokerage firms, credit card companies, money market funds, mutual funds, investment banks, and hedge funds.

Over the past 40 years, the financial structure has expanded greatly in two ways. One way is the types of products and services offered. The second is that the financial industry now plays a much larger role in the economy than it did 40 years ago. That growth required three conditions: (1) changes in government financial regulations, (2) capabilities in information technology, and (3) government policy favoring low interest rates and increasing debt. Note that two of the three factors came from government policy.

The most obvious result coming from the growth of the financial structure was a large increase in debt: federal government, local government, and private. As explained above using simple examples, debt under our current monetary structure tends to cause distortions in the economic structure and to increase economic inequality. The increasing inequality comes from two things. First, there is the direct effect of inflation. Second, the distortions to the economic structure tend to be unfavorable to the lower socioeconomic class.

What we've covered so far are the more or less direct effects on the economic structure resulting from the policies and functioning of the banking system and the derived financial system. From that same perspective, we now look briefly at some of the effects on the social structure. Following that, we will take up the perspective of government spending and look at how it affects the economic and social structures.

Under our current system, which discourages saving and encourages borrowing, the age-old virtue of thrift has been denigrated. In the gold society, savers had high confidence in obtaining two benefits. First, they could lend money at a fair return. Second, their saved money would grow in value rather than decline. Those expectations are exactly opposite under today's monetary structure. The absence of thrift in a society will ultimately have a negative effect. For particular circumstantial reasons discussed previously in this book, the United States was able to delay some of those effects and is just now beginning to experience them.

A less obvious social effect resulting from the broken link between savers and borrowers is that this also weakened a linkage that historically existed in all societies between the older and younger generations. Typically, older people had a higher ratio of savings to earned income than did younger people. The younger could borrow from the older, which established both an economic and social link between the generations. While this transaction still happens, it is far from the normal situation.

An ever-cheapening dollar and a continuously growing debt result in a social fixation on money that is different than a concern for money that is limited to earning what is required to live and to save for the future. Rather, this fixation happens because of the uncertainty of the value of money, a recognition of the capricious nature of a fiat monetary structure. The fixation is amplified because at the same time we entered a fiat structure, we also entered a new condition in the social structure: retirement. Never before has an entire society had the possibility of living 20 to 30 years after a person quits working. One result of this fixation (and desperation) is attempting to compensate by "investing" in housing and the stock market. However, both of those assets depend to a large extent upon the fiat money system for increased prices.

We noted above that our monetary structure tends to accelerate the pace of change compared to what it would be in the reference (gold) society. This ever-faster rate of change has a profound impact on the social structure. One of them was discussed in an earlier chapter, namely, it contributes to the creation of a disoriented psychological state I called *anomie*. We simply can't keep up. The second impact is the contribution to moral quandaries that are unknowingly created—hidden as an unintended side effect of the monetary structure—but which will eventually have to be addressed. Indeed, they are now becoming unavoidable. Some of these will be explored in the next part of the book.

Now, we switch perspectives from the banking system to government spending and again look at the effects on economic and social structures. Larger government deficits and therefore larger government debt is built upon the monetary structure and the banking system, as explained above. But government spending has its own effect independent of the direct banking system effects. That is what we will consider now. In this chapter, the conceptual basis for these effects is what we will discuss. Several particular examples will be addressed in detail in the next part.

In any society, government necessarily possesses power. It can pass laws and regulations. But government is limited by resources. The more resources it obtains by whatever means, the greater its power over both the economic and social structure. The founders of the United

States recognized the tendency for power to be abused and therefore instituted additional checks and balances on power. An important component of that protection was the creation of somewhat autonomous state governments under the federal government. This structure not only limited power, it also allowed different states to experiment with different approaches and to accommodate regional preferences of citizens. As we shall see, under our current monetary structure, all three functions of state government—limiting central power, experimentation, and regional preferences—have been compromised.

The growth of size and power of the federal government in its own right, plus the compromising of state power and functions, were possible because of our fiat monetary structure. It is this additional power made possible by the monetary structure that is the subject of this chapter.

Again, we will contrast the gold society with our current society to help explain the concepts.

A number of those concepts can be illustrated with one example. Assume a society decides that some people who are not working should receive money through a social welfare program. This program is not for the temporarily unemployed; that is a separate program. This new program is for those who cannot or do not work. The government creates a social welfare program for doing so. How does this play out in each society?

In the gold society, the government has two options. It can raise taxes or it can reduce spending somewhere else. Let's assume that society has voted that this should be an additional program. Therefore, taxes are increased. The next decision is when the social welfare payments should begin. One option is to delay the start until sufficient taxes have been gathered and set aside for that purpose. A second option is for the legislation to have authorized initial borrowing so that the program can be started immediately. In this case, the new taxes will need to be slightly higher in order to pay for the interest on the loan. The government then becomes a borrower, just like in the examples above. They offer bonds at interest rates that will attract savers to purchase the bonds.

In the gold society, it is clear to everyone what the program costs. Thus, social pressure encourages fellow citizens to minimize their claims for these welfare payments. That is, the person claiming such benefits is acutely aware that his neighbor is paying taxes to fund it. Nonetheless, imagine that an increasing number of people apply for welfare payments and as a result the program has insufficient funds. Citizens must now decide if taxes should be raised again or if the rules need to be tightened so that overall payments remain within budget. For example, if the citizens do not want to pay more taxes, they may vote to reduce the amount of payments or make it more difficult to qualify for them.

If our reference society, the gold society, is large, this program may be administered at the state level. Each state could have different rules for their program, would collect their own taxes, and would have local oversight on conformity to the rules. The key point is this. In the gold society, however administered, there is visibility and tight control on the program.

In today's fiat monetary structure, the situation plays out much differently. As already noted, many of our social programs started or were dramatically expanded in the 1960s. This was done by creating money. Citizens didn't consider either the current cost or the long-term costs of the programs. The money simply appeared over time as increased debt. The process happened repeatedly in the following decades. Expansions to welfare programs were never voted on explicitly. They continued to grow because the real costs were masked in a huge federal budget and by increased debt and inflation. In today's system, the program is neither visible nor controlled.

What happens to the economic and social structure in each case? In the gold society, the cost of the welfare program is totally paid at each point in time. No debt is incurred that has to be paid by future generations. The citizens know that part of the income from their labor is being taxed for the purpose of supporting fellow citizens who need help. Because of this visibility and control, the society will continually invest effort to minimize the number of people who need help. The economic structure will adjust to employ as many people as possible. Efforts will be made—very likely with no appeal for yet more taxes—to provide training for employment for the most disadvantaged in society. Charitable organizations will play a role in this process. Those who need help will see the economic and social effort invested on their behalf by their fellow citizens and will therefore be motivated to do their part in preparing for employment.

In today's system, every aspect of the situation is different, and in some cases exactly opposite. Those who receive the welfare payments are, of course, consuming goods and services that must be produced by other citizens, but the cost or extra burden is not easily recognized, as it is in the gold society. Therefore, society is missing the social and economic pressure that would motivate adjustments—that is, the feedback is missing. Most of the purchasing power for the welfare payments comes by increasing debt rather than truly settling the expenses at the time of consumption. As a result, three things happen. First, some of the true cost is postponed for later generations to pay. Second, all of the citizens will pay a price because of price inflation generated by the created money. Third, all citizens present and future must pay interest on the debt. Whereas in the gold society the tax was present and explicit, in today's society the tax gets hidden in two ways: 1) part of the tax is deferred for future generations to pay, 2) part of the tax is hidden in price inflation.

Not surprisingly, in the absence of instructive feedback, the number of people who received welfare payments and the total amount paid steadily increased. The economic structure must adjust to the reduced number and type of workers. However, the impact on society goes far beyond the direct economic accommodations. Our social structure is altered when the connection between consumption and production is damaged. Family structure and dynamics change in ways that diminish the development of children into young adults who can be productive citizens. All of this works together to create widening inequality, a subject examined in detail in the next part of the book.

Because the monetary structure has allowed the federal government to step in and alleviate the immediate symptoms of economic and social stress, our social structure has undergone a big change. For many people, the first thought for a solution to a problem is to look to government rather than to family, community, or charitable organizations.

Of the multiple other examples we could discuss related to the tremendous power that flows to the federal government under our monetary system, only two will be mentioned briefly. Because the federal government can offer created money to the states, there is a tendency for the federal government to take over and centralize government functions. This reduces the competition of new ideas and new approaches. It also minimizes respect for regional differences. A good example is the educational system. The second type of example involves the federal government favoring some types of businesses and punishing other types. Both of these will be explored in the next part of the book.

A final observation to close this chapter. In the last fifty years, each time the government felt it necessary to respond to some economic event, and there have been multiple such events, the attempt to fix something has always been directed at the financial structure, never at the fundamental basis of our monetary structure.

RULERSHIP STRUCTURE

"Rank does not confer privilege or give power. It imposes responsibility."
Peter Drucker

"The man of system . . . is apt to be very wise in his own conceit; and is often so enamoured with the supposed beauty of his own ideal plan of government, that he cannot suffer the smallest deviation from any part of it . . . He seems to imagine that he can arrange the different members of a great society with as much ease as the hand arranges the different pieces upon a chess-board. He does not consider that in the great chess-board of human society, every single piece has a principle of motion of its own, altogether different from that which the legislature might choose to impress upon it."
Adam Smith

We opened this part of the book with a chapter titled, "Thinking Like a Ruler." In that chapter we looked at the implicit bargain in which citizens relied upon "government" to govern society. That arrangement was compared to the owners of a company who hired a management team to run the company and thereafter paid little attention to how it was run. Just as the owners eventually recognized that their company was in trouble and they would have to take full responsibility for it, we as citizens are now coming to terms with the reality that the implicit bargain did not work out well. In our analogy, the owners of the company faced the difficult prospect of understanding what the real state of the company was, how it got there, and what must be done to restore its value and profitability. The owners realized they not only had to accept more responsibility, they had to learn a great deal about how to operate the company, things they previously trusted the management to do. As citizens, we must now do the same for the rulership of our society.

Preceding chapters presented some of what citizens must know as they take on their new role. We looked at concepts and facts that help explain why and how things happened as they did. A common thread through those chapters was feedback: what feedback we saw and did not see, what was properly understood and what was misunderstood, and how we were able to temporarily mitigate and postpone some of the consequences of our actions.

In this chapter, we look at our rulership structure: how it was shaped, what resulted from it, and the changes it is currently undergoing.

In any society, given its worldview, the well-being of citizens depends to a large extent upon the wisdom, knowledge, and concern of the rulership. This is true no matter the form of rulership (government). Almost all people throughout the history of civilization have lived under worldviews, and therefore forms of government, that divide society into the rulers and the ruled. Under those circumstances, the general citizenry often had little opportunity to provide feedback to rulers. In many cases, the only form of feedback available was rebellion, which carried the risk of a violent response from rulership.

Democracy, at least as practiced in the United States, completely changes two of the characteristics noted above. First, there is not an exclusive ruling class. A person who is a regular citizen one day may as a result of an election be part of the rulership tomorrow. Second, feedback from citizens to rulers is an essential characteristic of democracy. Every two years, citizens have the opportunity to keep or replace a portion of those holding rulership positions. This feedback, which can alter government, is done peacefully without fear or coercion on the part of rulers or citizens.

However, those differences between a democracy and other forms of rulership cannot negate principles. The well-being of citizens still depends upon the wisdom, knowledge, and concern of the rulers. This brings us to one of the core concepts of this book. Each citizen, whether or not they ever apply for any position related to rulership, must still simultaneously function in two roles. One of those roles, of course, is that of a regular citizen going about their daily lives. The second role needs clarification. It would be simple to say that the second role is as ruler, but that could be misleading. The vast majority of citizens will never run for an elected office nor will they hold an unelected, upper-level position in one of the government agencies. Most citizens will never actually have their hands on the levers of power. Consequently, the second role for most citizens is to select those who will wield direct rulership power. Here, the analogy from the first chapter works well. The second role is analogous to that of the owners of the company who realized that it is their responsibility, and theirs alone, to select managers. In the governance of society, citizens are selecting rulers rather than managers, of course, but society will only work well and be "profitable" to the extent that citizens do a good job of selecting rulers.

We must pause to acknowledge a fact that follows from the above discussion. The problems facing our society today must largely be attributed to the wisdom, knowledge, and concern of citizens as exercised over the last seventy years. One way to view the implicit bargain that formed between citizens and the "management" class is that both groups assumed the management class could bear most of the responsibility for the wisdom, knowledge, and concern necessary to govern society successfully. In today's vernacular, we might say that too much of such capacity was outsourced to the management class. Now that we know this arrangement did not work out as well as everyone hoped, it is necessary to reevaluate what is meant by "wisdom, knowledge, and concern" and how the associated responsibilities should be allocated between regular citizens and rulership.

In previous chapters, we've discussed the multiple ways in which the world was new and different in the middle of the last century when the implicit bargain began forming. As a result, mental models about how the world was going to work were much different than such models only fifty years before. If just one statement could be used to describe that model, it would be this: society can be scientifically managed. That model held certain perspectives—again, mostly implicit—toward wisdom, knowledge, and concern. Some oversimplified observations will help explain those perspectives.

Knowledge tended to mean those things that were necessary for scientific management. Technique, process, science, and "scientific" models were the primary ingredients of *knowledge*. The objective was to have models for the behavior of people economically and socially. *Wisdom*, an element held in high regard a century earlier, was held in less esteem in favor of knowledge and management. Perspectives on *concern* are more subtle. Americans have always cared about their fellow citizens. That was still true in the middle of the twentieth century.

However, practical perspectives on *concern* were different. Again acknowledging the simplification, *concern* of fellow citizens had two core assumptions. First, there was a great deal of optimism about the economic and social future. Opportunity was available for everyone, meaning that each person could—and was expected to—care for themselves. Second, for the small percentage of people who could not succeed, or at least survive, in this new world, the government would see to their care.

During this time of transition, in which we are coming to terms with the reality that our previous approaches have brought us to this point and must be modified for the future, particular attention must be given to these three characteristics of rulership: wisdom, knowledge, concern.

In the chapter "Social Structure," we considered in some detail what all of the newness of the mid-twentieth century meant for human action. Increasing prosperity and freedom opened the way for the higher motivations of the Maslow hierarchy and did so at the same time that previous beliefs and structures which informed the *shoulds* and *should nots* of society were losing influence. Out of this new milieu came altered meanings for two words that are hugely important in discussing rulership structure: freedom and equality.

At one time, freedom meant that a person had the right to live a well-ordered life, to live in pursuit of the best ideals, and to do so without coercion by government or other groups in society. Freedom in that context could only be understood by recognizing that freedom requires responsibilities for oneself and for others in society. This understanding of freedom prevailed from before the founding of America up to the middle of last century. Then, under the many "newness factors" already discussed, the meaning of freedom began taking a more individualistic turn. The trend was to increase attention on personal goals and desires and to decrease attention on the responsibility to community and broader society.

In both the social and economic domains, the claim to "freedom" was made to enable and justify new behavior, some of which brought costs that were initially difficult to discern. Let's briefly look at simple examples to illustrate the point.

Some people wanted "freedom" to mean the removal of constraints on personal and social relationships. One area in which this new "freedom" was directed was sexual and family issues. As a consequence, over time, increasing numbers of children became part of family situations that provided inadequate economic support and inadequate development and training in order to become productive citizens. Government responded by subsidizing the associated costs through direct financial aid and additional social services.

Something analogous happened with "economic freedom." Over time, a theory of business emerged in which maximizing profit was the primary objective and was increasingly pursued by passing some costs to others. Once again, government stepped in to cover those costs, one example being by direct financial aid and social services directed at lower-paid individuals.

Eventually, some citizens wanted *freedom* to mean protection from the hardships and uncertainties of life. Through the political process (politicians making promises), "the government" attempted to meet their desire.

Note what happened as personal and economic "freedoms" expanded in ways that weakened or severed the benefit-responsibility and behavior-consequence linkages. First, we recognize that such linkages cannot be broken without costs. Second, we recognize that the costs associated with these "freedoms" were socialized. That is, they were transferred from the primary actors to society as a whole.

Democracy depends on a particular meaning of *equality*. At the time of our founding, this meaning of equality would be stated as equality under the law or equality under God. Until the middle of last century, this was the prominent meaning of equality and remains important today. We will discuss it in detail shortly, but first we need to look at a couple of meanings of equality that have become increasingly important since the 1950s.

The simplest of those two additional meanings is often referred to as equal outcomes and contrasted with equal opportunity. For a person who believes that equality means equal outcomes, society has an obligation to pass laws that minimize the differences among citizens. Of course, wide variations are possible in exactly what differences should be addressed and what *minimize* means in a particular context. As discussed in earlier chapters, any attempts to bring about equal outcomes must by definition require diminishing freedom. However, in recent decades, some have argued that the trade-off is worthwhile. We will look at specific examples in the next part of the book.

Interestingly, the "freedoms" discussed above resulted in some groups being disadvantaged in the ability to use equal opportunity to achieve equal outcomes. The government attempted, yet again, to mitigate those disadvantages with more policies and programs, the costs of which were also socialized.

The second additional meaning of equality has to do with opinions and ideas. As discussed in the "Social Structure" chapter, the declining influence of Christianity and other sources of moral authority together with the rise of thinking that held there is no such thing as right and wrong or true and false or good and bad brought about a growing belief that nothing is objective. Everything is relative to a person's private understanding and experience, and subjective in the sense that each person's opinion or assessment is as good as—that is, equal to—that of any other person.

Under this umbrella of subjectivism and relativism, and with the elevation of personal autonomy, this aspect of the meaning of equality is illustrated by statements such as, "I'm as good as you are" or, "My opinion is equal to yours." But, of course, that cannot be true. Whatever the reasons, some people are more intelligent, more courageous, more virtuous, more kind, and so on than average. Likewise, some assessments and opinions are closer to reality and more likely to be of value than others. Taken far enough, this view of equality, which is increasingly common today, creates an environment in which one person says to another, "You have no right to encourage me to improve because my ways and my understanding are as good as yours." The corollary result is that a person who sees another acting in harmful ways is reluctant to suggest a better alternative because, the thinking goes, "I have no right to offer insight to another person."

These two meanings, equality of outcomes and equality of opinions, have influenced government policy. Compared to decades ago, policymakers are more inclined to support programs that create illusions of equality of outcomes and compensate for behavior that flows from the belief that all opinions and ideas are equal. Examples include policies that ignore the value of a nuclear family, that assume all children should be treated the same in school, that citizens should not be held personally responsible for productive employment, or that all risks in life can be prevented or ameliorated by government. All such programs, of course, require resources. Therefore, what was said about the costs associated with new meanings of *freedom* can be said of *equality*: the costs are not fully borne by the primary actors but are socialized.

In order to socialize costs, the government must use some mechanism by which society in whole pays for the costs. Elsewhere, we've looked at several such mechanisms: debt to pass the costs to later generations, formal tax increases, taxation through inflation, and higher prices for goods and services to pay for regulations. Whatever the details, the decision to socialize costs both engages and alters the rulership structure.

As we saw in earlier chapters, this socializing of costs was possible because of a changing monetary and financial structure coupled with unique domestic and world events.

Now we take up the meaning of equality that is most fundamental to a democracy: equality under the law. In order to explain a new dimension, or a newly important dimension, of equality under the law, we will look at it from two perspectives. The first perspective is the traditional one of equal standing and equal treatment under the law. It deals with the actual execution, what happens in practice, with regard to equality under laws that all citizens agree are proper. Even in this traditional perspective, new things are happening. The second perspective is new and deals with laws for which there is sharp disagreement among citizens regarding their propriety because of different worldviews or values. I will refer to these perspectives respectively as execution and worldview.

Before discussing the specifics of each perspective, it will be helpful to summarize some points from earlier chapters, that apply to both perspectives.

A sense of what *is* just and fair and a strong need *for* justice and fairness are part of human nature. Yet history shows that regardless of the form of rulership, regardless of the prevailing worldview, justice and fairness are difficult to obtain. Of all forms of government, democracy most depends upon justice and fairness. Democracy is built on the concept of "equal under the law." However, even under democracy, those lofty goals are not achieved. Why is that true?

As with so many questions of society, the answer lies in human nature. The same human nature that desires justice and fairness also possesses such characteristics as favoritism, greed, and fear, which work against consistent and universal justice and fairness. People who are poor or who lack connections to those in power or who belong to out-of-favor groups are more likely to be denied treatment that is just and fair.

Citizens understand that justice and fairness are ideals that can never be achieved perfectly in any society. As long as the effort is ongoing within society to work toward those ideals, and as long as the sense of injustice and unfairness remains low, the society can function well. However, when enough citizens believe that the current circumstances are not acceptable and that, furthermore, the trend is toward decreasing justice and fairness—that is, when a "fairness" threshold has been reached—the society will undergo an adjustment process. Depending on the specific characteristics of the society at that time, such adjustments may be orderly and beneficial or they may be disruptive and ultimately harmful.

Now we are ready to take up the "execution" perspective on equality under the law.

For the purposes of this chapter, the key point—and the reason for the word "execution"—is that for most of the history of the United States the struggle within society was not about the intent or content of the laws. Almost every citizen easily accepted the premise and intent of the laws. The struggle, and sometimes the conflict, came because some people were not treated as justly and fairly as others. Stated from a negative view, some people were effectively denied equal treatment. Many related details have been the subject of social and political debate for decades, but those details won't be discussed here.

Instead, I want to focus on the fact that the struggle and debate have broadened and gathered fuel from broad inequalities in society that go beyond a circumscribed "equality under the law." In recent years, parts of society are operating very close to that fairness threshold. As a result, we now witness disruptive behaviors and attitudes. We will look at some of these later.

Because it is new, we need to develop some background for the "worldview" perspective on equality under the law

From its founding, America has been characterized as a country accepting of diverse people. Our ability to assimilate people from different backgrounds is one of the reasons for America's strength and success. However, our Founders also recognized that factions naturally develop within a free society and that if those factions became powerful, democracy would be threatened. In fact, the mitigation of the influence of factions was a major concern throughout the development of our founding documents. That is, diversity and commonality are in tension and must be kept in appropriate balance.

With the benefit of hindsight, we now see that it was not diversity as such that was beneficial in the development of America; it was diversity *within* a certain sphere. People came to America because they believed in its ideals and wanted to benefit from the opportunities offered by the American way. They wanted to "be American." The incoming diversity would not have been helpful if, for example, those coming in were intent upon destroying American ideals and opportunity.

Furthermore, for most of our history, those who came to America shared many aspects of a common worldview. The diversity and pluralism represented among incoming people tended to be differences within a common view of how society should work and, maybe more importantly, a shared set of values. There was diversity within a shared worldview. This common understanding together with the political safeguards implemented by the Founders allowed the "melting pot" of America to realize the benefits of diversity while avoiding the destruction of powerful factions.

(The worldview of a society includes the values it holds. I list them separately at times to emphasize that social stress and conflict are most often caused when there is a conflict of values or when values are threatened.)

This is now changing. A weakening of our shared worldview was evident several decades ago. Over the past couple of decades, this weakening has accelerated and has now reached the level of beginning disintegration. In some cases, this disintegration is extreme, where one group holds some portion of its worldview and some of its values in direct contradiction to another group. Such a condition is socially unstable.

As a society, we are dealing with several converging currents: (1) increasingly serious social and economic problems with no solutions in view, (2) diverging—sometimes conflicting—values and views of how society should function, (3) growing capacity for human action coincident with diminishing guidance on how we should act. And all of this is happening in a world that is changing ever faster. In the "Social Structure" chapter, I suggested that the influence of these currents together with other stressors has induced the disordered state of anomie, a condition that amplifies all that is negative and hinders the spirit of cooperation and reason, which are essential for any path to solutions.

What results are coming out of this milieu? The first observation is that debate, persuasion, and compromise—all hallmarks of effective democracy—have been rendered ineffective. As such, solutions are not possible. As problems grow and as new circumstantial stresses arise, the status quo becomes unacceptable. A race for power begins because each competing group sees the only possible path forward as gaining control of the federal government. The race for power induces fear among the different groups. The natural progression of an unchecked race for power is for each group to find ways to suppress or coerce other groups. Of course, each such effort increases fear and concern, and the efforts accelerate.

Coercion is the pivot point. When one group is willing to impose their values or their ideas of how society should function upon other groups who hold opposing values and ideas, fear and conflict can only escalate. In this environment, one group uses positive law to purposefully override what the other group holds as natural law. "Equality under the law" has no useful meaning under these conditions. If the process of coercion is not stopped, our society will fracture. The particular characteristics of the fracturing can't be predicted. That is, the details of government and social life can't be predicted. However, what can be predicted is that the resultant society will not be a free society in any way in which freedom has been understood over the past several hundred years.

The domain of rulership would be further complicated because only autocrats or would-be dictators, not capable leaders, will be willing to step forward. Returning to a key theme of this book, the future of our rulership structure—and thus the future of our society—depends on ordinary citizens quickly accepting that only our collective wisdom, knowledge, and concern can first stop and then reverse what is happening.

Part III

STRUCTURAL BASIS OF INEQUALITY

"For instance, it is thought that justice is equality, and so it is, though not for everybody but only for those who are equals; and it is thought that inequality is just, for so indeed it is, though not for everybody, but for those who are unequal."
Aristotle

"An imbalance between rich and poor is the oldest and most fatal ailment of all republics."
Plutarch

INEQUALITY

"From the protection of different and unequal faculties of acquiring property, the possession of different degrees and kinds of property immediately results; and from the influence of these on the sentiments and views of the respective proprietors, ensues a division of the society into different interests and parties."
James Madison

". . . any activity of the government deliberately aiming at material or substantive equality of different people, . . . must lead to the destruction of the Rule of Law."
F. A. Hayek

Much of our political debate today has to do with some form of inequality. In some cases, the issue of inequality may be explicit. For example, the meaning of *inequality* most likely to come to mind is economic: the fact that the distribution of wealth and income among groups is widening. But our problems of inequality are broader than simply economic. In other cases, the explicit problem receiving attention may be driven by underlying inequalities, an example of which is education.

However, we know that inequalities (that is, differences) always exist within a society. Such differences are a consequence of human nature. Our attributes, our abilities, our personalities, and our goals and desires vary widely. Therefore, in any society, especially a free society, differences exist.

Social and personal problems can arise from these differences for three reasons. (1) Fairness. Some causes of these differences are judged to be unfair. That is, some aspects of the structures of society tend to favor or disfavor one group over another. (2) Expectations. People have expectations that go unmet for reasons they did not anticipate or cannot control. (3) Psychology. Multiple studies indicate that some people will choose a state in which in absolute terms they are worse off but in relative terms are above the average of their community or society. For example, a person might prefer to earn $50,000 a year if the average in their community is $30,000 over the case in which they earn $80,000 when the average is $100,000—even though their material well-being is much higher in the second case.

This chapter deals with reasons (1) and (2) because they are caused by decisions made by society as a whole and are amenable to improvement by votes of the people. Reason (3) comes from human nature and from worldview elements shaping what a society values, how it defines virtue, and how it views hierarchy. It is not addressed in this chapter because it is not amenable to change by voting, at least not in the short-term.

We begin by considering conditions that cause differences and are judged as unfair. If each citizen thought the distribution of resources and opportunities was fair, there would be no political contention about unfair differences.

Every society has its own views of how the world works and of how it judges fairness. What is considered desirable in one society may be undesirable in another. From its founding, citizens of the

United States have supported the idea that hard work, risk-taking, and luck will result in unequal distributions, but those distributions would generally be assessed as fair as long as 1) a person is not intentionally restrained from succeeding, and 2) the general level of prosperity continues to increase. In recent decades, the support for those ideas and the reality of those conditions have deteriorated.

Today, different groups of citizens see a lack of fairness in a range of circumstances. In addition to the distribution of wealth and income, this includes fairness in who receives government aid and who does not. For example, consider a family with one or more members earning an income, maybe one person holding more than one job. That income places the family in the higher portion of "lower income" or in the bottom portion of "middle income." They struggle to make ends meet. This working family observes another household with no one earning a living, yet because it receives various forms of government assistance has a standard of living approximating that of the working family. The working family sees this as unfair.

We can't properly understand the social problem we call *inequality*—differences in outcomes judged as unfair—without revisiting some economic principles. Economic freedom was required for the tremendous increase in material well-being in the past seventy years. Division of labor (specialization) and the necessary accumulation of capital was the engine that produced material prosperity. Freedom and specialization provide the environment in which people can most fully exercise or express their abilities and goals. All of those things contribute to material prosperity. However, by their nature, they highlight the differences among people. At any point in time, some individuals possess a set of attributes that make them highly productive (in an economic sense) to society. They will receive more income and accumulate more wealth than the average citizen.

The economic processes, the engine of prosperity, began more than 150 years prior to 1950, the beginning of our reference timeframe. Thus, Americans have been familiar with these economic realities for many generations. However, in recent decades, for reasons addressed in earlier chapters, more and more Americans began to see not only larger differences in outcomes but differences that were not fair. It is this reality that has made *inequality* the political issue it is today.

As a reminder, all of the assessments of unfairness depend partly upon measurements. As we saw in the "Economic Structure" chapter, great care is required to accurately understand measurements. All measurements in society, economic or otherwise, are subject to errors, assumptions, and biases. This is true of measurements used in the debate about inequality. Things are not always as they appear; opinions and data presented in the public debate are often incomplete or inaccurate. We need measurements, of course, but they should be rigorously confirmed, from the ground up, by independent groups.

Cause

With the above understanding, it is clear that our investigation of fundamental causes must be directed primarily at the assessment of unfairness and secondarily at the differences as such. For example, a spread of incomes measured as X may be judged as fair or not fair depending on the broader circumstances in society.

Any understanding of fundamental causes must begin with fundamental principles. From our study of human nature in the first part of the book we know several things. In any society some people will have both a strong desire for power and the necessary attributes to acquire it. When that desire for power is strong enough and when the moral development is weak enough, some people will be willing not only to be unfair but will intentionally violate rights in order to obtain and retain power. A concentration of power, especially in government but also in industry, will always result in favor to those at the top and disfavor to those at the bottom.

When the power structures within a society, and most importantly the rulership structure, become strong enough, the number of acts and circumstances judged as unfair will increase. This has a corrosive effect upon society because other citizens will come to understand that in order to succeed, or simply to protect their interests, they must acquiesce to or participate in laws and processes that contribute to unfairness.

It is for reasons of human nature that a society that wishes to remain free and prosperous must contain checks and balances on power. In addition, the society must have a vigilant citizenry with proper understanding. Both of those requirements were well known by and of primary concern to the Founders of the United States. They built protections in the Constitution; they advised their generation and the ones to follow that only a moral and virtuous people could keep the freedoms Americans possessed.

What criteria are to be used in judging what is right and fair? Returning again to principles, the worldview of a society provides the criteria. Specifically, its belief system (religion), its values, and its understanding of economic laws are the components of a worldview that most strongly influence the assessment of fairness.

In the first two parts of the book, we explored how the proper understanding and vigilance of citizens has diminished. We also saw that our belief system has changed and that our traditional belief system, Christianity, lost influence. As a result, some of our values have changed or, at a minimum, their importance and ranking have changed. Finally, those changes together with rapidly changing internal and external environments brought about a distorted understanding of our economic system.

Bringing these elements together, we can summarize as follows. Today, our circumstances present problems and processes that need to be reassessed in terms of fairness. At the same time, our criteria and understanding for making such assessments have changed much since 1950—and there are growing differences among citizens over those criteria and understandings.

We need another component to understand assessments of unfairness. There appears to be a law of human nature, or at least a rule of modern times, which is that unmet expectations cause problems. This is true in personal relationships, business relationships, and social relationships. Although our expectations may have been moderated somewhat following 2008, they are still very high. Understanding our expectations and why they may not be met is an important part of comprehending why more Americans are judging more circumstances as unfair.

Two points underlie much of our expectations. First, unique world circumstances following World War II were extremely favorable for the United States. Such circumstances are no longer true. Second, because the United States controlled the world's monetary system, we were able to (1) postpone and mitigate adjustments and consequences of policy and structure, and (2) borrow heavily. Thus, we lived beyond our means, pushing the costs to later generations— now being paid in our time.

In this chapter, we will look at the creation of expectations. The most important point is that success came to be largely defined as material well-being, which is equivalent to defining success as a growing income and a growing accumulation of wealth. This definition of success has been reinforced by all forms of media, both in content and advertisements.

For many Americans, the media is now the dominant factor in their understanding of reality and of how the world works. It is therefore the dominant shaper of expectations. The influence of media has steadily grown for decades as its volume and ubiquity have increased and as other informing and mediating institutions have seen their influence decline. In recent decades, the impact of media was greatly amplified by new technology and new communication platforms. Statistics on the number of hours spent each day in the consumption of media are staggering. The challenges associated with this new configuration were discussed in an earlier chapter.

With media as the dominant informant, a person might easily think that most Americans enjoy a level of material success far above what is actual. The misunderstanding goes beyond material success because people are portrayed—or portray themselves—as happier and more satisfied than they really are. Finally, a person whose understanding of our economic system comes from popular media is likely to have a wrong understanding that will distort expectations about what is economically and financially possible.

It is objectively true that throughout American history each generation could assume the following generation would have a better life, even if the definition of *better* changed over time.

Another expectation, one that is brand new in history, is the concept of retirement in which the average citizen hopes to enjoy a high quality of life for two or three decades after they quit working. Stated plainly, the expectation is that a person can work for four decades and then live well for another two or three decades without working. This expectation developed over a couple of generations that were fortunate enough to retire at a time when productivity growth, demographics, and America's economic position in the world made this possible. The expectation remains one of the most powerful in our society, and is constantly reinforced by media, especially advertisements.

The United States is in the process of coming to terms with the reality that the expectations of many citizens won't be realized. Given current circumstances, the arithmetic suggests it is not possible. This reality alone helps explain an important cause for assessments of unfairness.

As a thought experiment, consider a whole segment of society that sees some evidence that their expectations will be met—at least, they find it believable. Yes, the group sees circumstances and behaviors that aren't ideal, and may not be truly fair, but it doesn't present a personal or social problem because they believe they personally are making progress. Then overnight something happens that makes it clear their expectations are not at all likely to be met and that the progress they thought they had already made is less than they had figured. Some percentage of the people in that segment of society will wake up the next day and feel strongly that circumstances are now unfair.

The 2008 financial crisis, the 2020 coronavirus pandemic, and the 2022 price inflation are examples of such "overnight" events.

Current Proposed Solutions

When something in our society is not working the way we want it to, we are motivated by human nature and our political process to find easily identifiable issues to blame. Almost always, such issues are not the real causes but are symptoms of more fundamental forces. Here are a few examples of culprits that have been blamed for our various problems: immigration, globalization, the elites, the rich, the educational system, and capitalism. When such targets are identified, we proceed to find ways to fix or remove these causes. Of course, trying to address a social problem by mitigating symptoms or by trying to fix intermediate causes one at a time will never produce a solution and, more often, will simply worsen the social problem and make it more difficult to solve in the future.

The purported cause most often addressed by government policy has to do with economic differences. Attempts at solutions frequently involve redistribution of income. An extreme example that has been part of political discussions in recent years is implementing a universal basic income (UBI). However, most redistribution programs tend to minimize personal responsibility and create incentives for not working.

Such programs do not provide real long-term solutions; they treat symptoms. In fact, they pose several challenges to a free society. First, though our monetary and financial structure has often hidden the reality, when people are given money for not working, it requires the taking of resources from those who are working to support those who are not. While transfer of resources is entirely appropriate in some cases within a society, our current programs and structures are not sustainable.

Second, redistribution programs, when they become unsustainable, generate social contention within society. This contention will lead to an unstable democracy if it persists. Third, unless administered with a great deal of wisdom, such transfer programs are an affront to human dignity. The implicit message is, "You can't contribute to society," or "Society does not need your contribution." Such understandings are damaging in any society but are particularly dangerous to stability in a society with universal suffrage. Furthermore, people want and need dignity, and a successful society needs human dignity. However, dignity can't be given or mandated; it comes from contribution.

These challenges were recognized by Franklin Roosevelt, who was arguably the father of America's social welfare system. In his 1935 State of the Union Address he said,

> *The lessons of history, confirmed by the evidence immediately before me, show conclusively that continued dependence upon relief induces a spiritual disintegration fundamentally destructive to the national fiber. To dole out relief in this way is to administer a narcotic, a subtle destroyer of the human spirit.*

Another approach to economic differences is to use laws and regulations requiring or prohibiting certain actions. This type of solution never works. Often, such laws and regulations offer advantages to the rich and powerful who can afford to work around them but work to the disadvantage of ordinary citizens and of smaller and less powerful entities. In some cases, this type of solution brings about larger problems. For example, the 2008 crisis was precipitated by the housing finance marketplace, which had been distorted by previous regulations encouraging or prohibiting how loans were made. Another common example is rent controls, which are implemented to make housing more affordable. The result, of course, is a reduced supply of housing and a reduced incentive for landlords to maintain their property.

In the next chapter, we will see how solutions based on education not only failed but created additional problems. We will also investigate this fact: inequality begins with the family you are born into.

Another approach, which only recently entered the public debate in a substantive way was to blame "capitalism" in general for all forms of inequality and to propose "socialism" as the solution. (I've used quotation marks to emphasize the poor definition of those words.) To propose socialism as a means of addressing inequality ignores all evidence of history, which teaches clearly that socialism tends to make the masses equally poor while the rulership structure becomes ever richer. This is the subject of an upcoming chapter.

Solution Framework

The social problem that goes under the name *inequality* is not a temporary condition of recent economic events or of the current political environment. It is perhaps the most serious domestic problem we face. In the words of Plutarch almost 2,000 years ago, "An imbalance between rich and poor is the oldest and most fatal ailment of all republics." Inequality (unfairness) destabilizes a society. Our situation may be more tenuous than anything Plutarch saw in his time because we have universal suffrage and ubiquitous, instantaneous communications—a reality unknown prior to the late twentieth century.

The fairness problem cannot be solved directly; it must be solved by changing the structures of society, which, in turn cannot be changed by isolated political "fixes." Nor is the solution, as some have recently suggested, to destroy current structures in the hope of rebuilding better ones. First, our structures encapsulate a great deal that is good and strong. Second, a society whose structures have been destroyed is more likely to disintegrate than to rebuild. Third, even if we did manage to rebuild structures following destruction of the old ones, the newly-rebuilt structures will produce the same types of problems (though perhaps manifested differently) unless we have a proper understanding of fundamental principles and of our present milieu.

Our path to a solution will be longer and more difficult than we might like. However, the good news is that along the path of addressing fairness, we will find solutions to many social challenges. That path begins with proper understanding.

Real solutions require that we wisely deal with fundamental principles. For the *fairness* problem, the first step is to accept differences in outcomes and circumstances that are inevitable in a free society. Society requires hierarchy. Some people must have more authority and more responsibility than others. As individuals, each person is different, having characteristics different from others. These personal differences influence the roles and responsibilities a person can assume in society. No process can undo these differences. Not everyone can be made into a superstar basketball player, not everyone can be CEO of a multinational corporation, not everyone can be a productive citizen by "following their dreams." Differences must be accepted. Differences as such are not unfair except perhaps in the sense behind the saying that "life is not fair."

Each person has roles to play in creating fairness in society. That is true for the rich and the poor, for those who have power and those who don't, those with advantages and those with disadvantages. Fairness is not something the rich and powerful create and then give to those who are poorer and have less power. Fairness is not something that can be coercively extracted from one group in favor of another.

As we've seen throughout this book, differences among citizens always exist. It has always been true no matter the society or the point in time. Some groups will hold more power in rulership, more control of resources, and more social influence than other groups. What determines the course of society is how those groups interact, and how they influence each other. Each group has responsibilities to other groups. Each group must accommodate the others. Today, in our country these relationships have deteriorated far enough that some people in one group hold in disdain some people in other groups. This situation cannot be sustained in a free society. Something will break. Properly understood, and under properly functioning structures, each group should appreciate what the other group contributes to society. No desirable future is possible without this understanding, appreciation, and respect.

Stated broadly, we have two main tasks. First, we must find a way to accept the realities discussed above, and we must find a way to regain our sense of roles, responsibilities, and respect necessary for a true society. These things are a first step, though we don't need to achieve them perfectly before we can make progress on the second step, which is to develop proper understanding and the requisite skills for restoring the feedback-adjustment process to its proper functioning. If this cycle is properly understood and not distorted or mitigated, we will be on the path of restoring the connection between benefit and responsibility, between behavior and consequences. And it is these mechanisms that will provide almost automatic guidance for the correction of problems in the structures of society.

Summary

In the previous part of the book, we focused on how a distorted feedback-adjustment process led to the distorted development of key structures in society. Many of our social problems today are the result of those distorted structures. One of those problems is commonly called *inequality*. That is, the distorted structures created the circumstances and processes that brought about the current level of differences and, more crucially, the reasons why those differences are judged as unfair. The progression went like this: because we improperly understood, improperly implemented, or simply ignored fundamental principles, we ended up with distorted structures. We must now work the process again, this time, with a proper understanding.

Finally, we the citizens must accept that our political, social, and economic votes are part of the cause and part of the explanation for whatever unfairness exists today. Our future votes will determine whether we find solutions.

In the next two chapters we consider two domains that contribute structurally to inequality: education and our economic system. The chapter on education is broader than what is commonly meant by the term. It is about the forming of a citizen. It is presented first to emphasize that it comes before and is more important than problems in our economic system, although we often assume that the latter is the origin of inequality.

Because recently *structure* and *structural* have been used by some groups to mean something quite different from what is meant in this book, I need to clearly define them. In this new usage, those terms seem to mean something impersonal and perhaps something to be destroyed by eliminating institutions or rewriting history or other extreme measures. That is not at all what is meant here. We recall that human action is what shapes society. Therefore, in this book, *structure* and *structural* mean the ways and means we as citizens have created—by our various types of voting—in order to carry out the functions of our society.

EDUCATION

"Education is simply the soul of a society as it passes from one generation to another."
G. K. Chesterton

"To educate a man in mind and not in morals is to educate a menace to society."
Theodore Roosevelt

Education is the answer; education cannot be the answer. The public school system can be fixed; the public school system is beyond repair. College for everyone is essential; college is becoming irrelevant. Such contrasting statements are vigorously debated. What is widely agreed is that no fundamental improvements have yet been made for decades—with each side blaming the other. What is going on? Why is this our present reality? This chapter will use principles and analyses from the first two parts of the book to show how we lost track of the fundamentals of education, and how we can properly understand the nature and role of education for our time.

Our first task must be to clarify language and meaning. One reason why the discussions are so confusing is that *education* has so many meanings and connotations that people may not be talking about the same thing even if they use the same words. On our way to more precise and therefore more useful terms, we will look at the role of "education" throughout history.

Let's begin by imagining a simple society with a simple economy in which no one is literate. What sort of training takes place? Each child will be instructed and formed in the ways of the culture. They will learn roles and responsibilities. They will be trained to develop their personal character. This will include the morals and virtues valued by society. They will be trained to contribute productively to society. We will group these aspects of training into three domains: *culture, character,* and *contribution*. Passing along from generation to generation what each of those domains demands from a member of society is essential if the society is to survive.

Every society depends on the development of the next generation, which of course means the training of children. This training could be described as follows. This is who we are. This is how things work. This is what we believe. These are your roles and responsibilities within society. These are the personal characteristics you need to develop.

Every society requires individuals who by early adulthood are capable of being productive and self-sustaining and possess the knowledge and character required of a citizen. The "required of a citizen" is especially important in a democratic society because political, economic, and personal liberty places great demands on its citizens, demands that must be met or the society will disintegrate.

While the detailed content of *culture, character,* and *contribution* varies by society, and may vary within a society over time, those essential categories are constant. The methods by which this training and development take place are also common through most of history. The development of a child was primarily in the hands of the family. Secondly, the community shaped the child. Most of the learning and training in all three domains was part of daily life. Most people learned how to make a living within the family or from on-the-job training, which in some cases involved a formal apprenticeship. An understanding of society's "who and what and why" was held in agreement by most people, who also felt it important to pass it on to the next generation.

However, in our time, the methods and means of training and development are radically changing from historical norms. Additionally, there is less agreement among citizens regarding "who and what and why." These changes are an important part of why "education" seems to be failing.

Because the development of the next generation determines the future, we should expect that what we call education played a critical role in creating our current circumstances. It follows that a reformed "education" is necessary as part of solutions to our social problems.

Because history matters, this chapter will establish the context of education in 1950 by looking at its development over the sixty years preceding 1950. Next, we will look at the economic and social influences that shaped education to the present day. With that background in hand, we will connect the outcomes of the resulting system to our present problems. Specifically, we will see how education (in the broad sense of the total development of young people) can be viewed as the social engine of unfairness (today's problem of inequality). Finally, we will conclude by thinking through elements of a solution framework.

By the beginning of last century, a shift was underway in the understanding of education. Formal education—that is, schooling in a classroom environment—was to become increasingly important. Formal schooling, which was not the norm for most people through most of history, was soon to become dominant. Well before the close of the last century, *education* usually meant what took place in a school. Furthermore, beginning in the middle part of the last century and steadily growing thereafter, the schools were performing duties beyond book learning. They were attempting to compensate for other changes in society.

We can't understand our current problems and therefore can't find solutions unless we grasp the changes that took place in the training and development of children in the last 100 years. Because *education* often has a more narrow meaning than in times past, I will use other words such as *training* and *development* along with *education*. *Schooling* means classroom-based training.

As described multiple times in earlier chapters, the world was hugely different in 1950 compared to the opening of the century. In this chapter we focus on those changes that most directly impacted the development of a child into early adulthood. The demand for schooling grew numerically and in the expectation of what schools should do. The traditional development environment was disrupted.

First, look at the numerical growth of schooling. In 1890 the number of students enrolled in high school was about 300,000 (0.5 percent of the population), whereas in 1950 the numbers were 6.4 million and 4.2 percent. Over those 60 years, the population increased by a factor of 2.4 while the number of students in high school increased by a factor of 21. Most of the demand for more schooling was driven by the changing characteristics of the economy; more of the jobs required more schooling. This growth put stress on the education system as it tried to expand the infrastructure and the number of teachers to meet the demand.

Second, the urbanization of America continued. In 1890, about 22 million people lived in urban areas, whereas in 1950 the number was 97 million (35% and 64% of the population respectively). A large percentage of that movement consisted of families or of young adults who would have children. An urban environment is a much different environment for development than traditional farming communities and small towns. Schools were soon trying to compensate for those differences, an effort that was in addition to keeping up with the numerical growth.

In this time of rapid transition, political and educational leaders had to make important decisions about the fundamental assumptions and objectives for the school system. There were two broad categories. In 1890, the beginning of our reference timeframe, the small percentage of people who completed high school tended to be naturally selected based on their interests and their ability. As a result, the curriculum and the standards could be higher and more uniform. Already by 1940, school officials could see that this would no longer be possible. They made decisions that started the path toward standardized curriculum and lower standards for everyone.

The second category of decision was what role schools should take in compensating for the absence of roles traditionally played by the community. An urban setting could not (or at least did not) have a way of replacing this developmental role that was so important. Leaders decided that the school system would attempt to fill those gaps.

As a result of those decisions and of how they were implemented, the middle decades of the twentieth century brought about fundamental changes to the development process of young people. For the first time in history, formal schooling was going to play a crucial role for an entire population (not just the elite class), supplanting the influence of community and other institutions. Formal schooling was now second only to the family in directing the development of a child.

With each passing decade, the demand for and upon schooling continued to grow. The reasons remained the same: economic and demographic. We now need to relate these changes and show their connection to our social problems today.

Economically, more and more employment opportunities were tied to the amount of schooling a person had. Employers had two reasons for requiring schooling. First, many jobs required more of the knowledge and skills obtained in schooling. Second, the attainment of a certain level of schooling is often a good indicator of other skills such as motivation, perseverance, and other soft skills a person acquires if they grow up in a nurturing environment.

As the economy grew, so did the demand for more people with more schooling. In addition, over several decades, the correlation grew between a person having more schooling and earning a higher income. In response, the demand for schooling increased even more. Initially, this demand caused more people to complete high school. This was followed by some high schools offering a richer set of programs so that some students would be better qualified than the average graduate. While the same thing took place at the college level, we will keep our focus on K-12 and take up college later.

As the economy was growing, its structure changed in ways that favored population centers. It was this economic reality that motivated the demographic change noted above: urbanization. This change continued for several decades following 1950. As a result, schools had to deal with an ever-increasing number of students who no longer grew up in a traditional community-based environment.

From 1950 to 1990 many women joined the workforce. The labor force participation of family-age women doubled in that period. As a result, many families had both parents working outside of the home. This had the effect of creating additional demand upon schools.

As noted in an earlier chapter, the traditional nuclear family began to break down at a faster rate in the second half of the twentieth century. A growing number of children were being raised in households that could not or would not guide the development of children in ways that were expected in previous generations.

Taken together, these demographic changes put demands upon schools that made them a different type of organization, a different environment, from what many Americans experienced prior to 1950. Today, schools are social service centers in addition to centers of learning. In many schools, teachers and administrators must invest a great deal of time and resources acting as surrogate parents. In some schools, more time and resources are spent on meeting the social and parental needs of children than are spent on classroom learning.

Given the history and circumstances described above, it is not surprising that the results of the schooling system are disappointing. For decades now, we as a society have decried the results and often blamed the schooling system. Blaming the schooling system alone is unfair, however. As a society, we have through our various modes of voting and through the implicit bargain discussed in the previous part of the book allowed the creation of our current system. We have given the schooling system the impossible task of compensating for problems in other structures of society, problems that have been growing for decades. Faced with an unrealizable task and blamed for the results, teachers and administrators are overwhelmed and frustrated. We will take this up later in the chapter when we look at perspectives on solutions.

If we can't put the blame for problems on the schooling system, where should we put it? In recognition that we must look at our problems as integrated and use fundamental principles both in understanding what happened and what we should do, I will make use of the term *preparation milieu*. I chose *preparation* to avoid commonly used words such as education, schooling, and training because they are so familiar and have so many connotations that it is easy to automatically assign a too narrow meaning. What we want to talk about is the total process of preparation of a young person to be a good citizen. Likewise, I chose *milieu* to avoid common words such as environment, system, and context. Furthermore, I use *milieu* in the broadest way to include not just physical systems and environments but also mental models and philosophies.

Preparation therefore includes what we've already talked about in different ways: (1) Training and passing along of *culture, character,* and *contribution*. (2) This is who we are. This is how things work. This is what we believe. These are your roles and responsibilities within society. These are the personal characteristics you need to develop. (3) Every society requires individuals who by early adulthood are capable of being productive, self-sustaining, and possessing the knowledge and character required of a citizen.

Milieu includes the family, community, schools, other organizations, and the media. It encompasses the principles, concepts, and opinions that society holds with regard to what exactly should be included in *preparation*. Milieu captures the specific objectives for the development of a person as well as what processes should be used and how they should work. The ideas (assumptions) that everyone can and should earn a roughly equivalent high school diploma and that schools can and should compensate for the diminishment of any other component of *preparation* are examples of what is included in *milieu*.

In the chapter "Social Structure," we looked at diverging components of worldviews, one of which was social values. Both the presence of the divergence as well as the particular characteristics of the divergence are an important element of *milieu* because they result in society having different goals and processes for *preparation*.

With the definition of *preparation milieu* in place, we can state an important fact: our preparation milieu is the primary driver of most of our problems carried under the label *inequality*. It is more foundational than the economic structure, though the latter is more often blamed. The preparation milieu has its effect along two primary paths. The first is objective and deals with what young adults know and believe, their character, their skills, and so on. That is, it deals with an assessment of the capacity to be a productive, self-sustaining person with the qualifications to be a good citizen. The nature and content of this path of influence was covered in previous chapters.

The second path of influence arose from the social splitting and sorting which were consequences of the objective deficiencies just noted. It is outside the scope of this book to look at all of the reasons and ways in which this took place. Here, we require only a broad sketch of what happened and of the effect upon society.

Earlier, we explored how distorted feedback-adjustment processes plus a lack of proper understanding together with the "implicit bargain" brought about changes in the structures of society. Those changes—most of which were unintended consequences—worked to the advantage of some and the disadvantage of others. As the structural changes developed, some citizens were able, by personal characteristics, luck, or whatever, to adapt well. Many prospered. The opposite was also true; some citizens were not in a position to adapt or adjust. Some in this group suffered ongoing loss of material and social well-being.

In what follows, we will simplify the discussion by looking at two groups of citizens. The "fortunate" group are those who prospered during this period of structural change while the "unfortunate" are those who suffered, often both materially and socially. Although many factors combined to determine who was likely to end up in the fortunate or unfortunate group, the most important determinant was the quality of their preparation milieu.

As the prosper-suffer differences between the fortunate and unfortunate groups grew, they separated in several ways. Those who were fortunate tended to marry from the same group; likewise for the unfortunate group. The fortunate group moved to school districts with good schools while the unfortunate group often stayed in place and watched their school districts decline. The fortunate avoided the negative effects of government policy while the unfortunate suffered unintended consequences. The fortunate group contained a much higher percentage of well-functioning, capable families while the unfortunate group experienced large increases in disintegrated and dysfunctional families. The process continues today.

Children from the fortunate group benefit from a preparation milieu that is much better than those experienced by children from the unfortunate group. As would be expected, this pattern is reinforced with one group doing better and better over time as the other group does poorer and poorer. Also as expected, the schools serving the districts with the most fortunate families are able to invest more resources into the preparation of students because they spend less resources on social services and surrogate parenting than do schools serving the unfortunate group. The reinforcing cycle operates quickly, meaning that the gap between the groups accelerates.

As a result, a growing number of people in the unfortunate group are not self-sustaining, let alone prepared for what is required of a citizen in a free society. Stated plainly, many who graduate high school are woefully underprepared for employment, for further training, and for the responsibilities of citizenship. Because the preparation milieu is foundational, any solution must begin with it. But our discussion of solutions will come later. For now, we turn our attention from the formational K-12 years to the preparation that occurs after high school.

After high school (AHS) will be used for any training that occurs following the K-12 period of development. *College* will be used when necessary to refer to degree-granting institutions. Thus, AHS encompasses on-the-job training, "technical" and "career" training in any field, as well as college.

Problems related to AHS are easier to understand and fix than those related to K-12. In fact, one of the major problems for AHS is the lack of preparedness of many who graduate high school. We will consider that problem later. Almost all other problems related to AHS are caused by misunderstandings brought about by decades of distorted feedback and adjustment.

Public discussions often focus on "college education" rather than the broad AHS domain. I will call this the "college problem." When we understand that problem, we will more clearly see the entire AHS picture. Before looking at the underlying causes, we will consider objective measures of what happened. Then we will investigate why.

One aspect of the "college problem" has analogies to the high school situation discussed above. During the same timeframe in which high school enrollment increased by 21 times, college enrollment increased by 15 times. However, while high school enrollment plateaued around 1970, college enrollment continued to grow. In the following 40 years to 2010, while the population increased by 50 percent, college enrollment increased by 160 percent. Colleges had to adjust to handle many more students and to deal with a wide range of abilities and interests.

However, a critical difference exists between K-12 and AHS. Whereas the entire domain of K-12 training is controlled by government funding, certification, and regulation, the situation is different for AHS. Attendance alone reveals much. In K-12, approximately 90 percent of all students are enrolled in public schools. In the AHS environment many students don't pursue AHS at all, and some get training from sources outside of traditional colleges. About 35 percent of graduating high school students enroll in a four-year college, but many of those don't graduate. For those who do attend college, they are in an environment in which government has less control over the philosophy and curricula. Thus, the AHS environment is more diverse and less controlled.

Why do we have the "college problem"? Why do many still believe that "college for everyone" is the solution to our economic (and therefore social) problems? Once again, we can turn to proper understanding and to the feedback-adjustment process for the answers.

Begin by considering a simple economic production system. Imagine that you are starting a business to produce many cakes every day. As your business grows, something happens in the broader economy that limits the supply of flour, your chief ingredient. At this point, your production of cakes is limited by the supply of flour. Therefore, the price of flour will go up. But the market will naturally adjust so that eventually plenty of flour is available and at a more attractive price. Flour will no longer limit your production. However, you would not say that flour caused your production (economic) growth. Rather, it was a resource that limited your production. When you can obtain all the flour you need, the availability of more flour does not necessarily mean you will produce more cakes.

In that simple example, no one would get confused and think that flour caused growth. But this type of confusion did take place during the economic growth in the decades following 1950. More people were obtaining more schooling at the same time that economic growth was continuing. The economy was changing in ways that required more people with more schooling. Because the need for schooled people was greater than the supply, they were paid more.

After a couple of decades of this trend, a confused idea developed. Rather than looking at people with a particular type of schooling as a necessary resource for the economy, it was thought that schooled people were causing economic growth—an example of confusing correlation with causation. This idea grew until it became widespread, so much so that government policy shifted toward encouraging college both in rhetoric and by subsidizing the cost of college. State governments funded college costs directly out of their budgets while the federal government subsidized indirectly through loans for students.

As a side note, long after many college degrees quit serving as an indicator of what a person knew, employers continued to use a degree as a criterion for hiring. One reason was that a college degree had some correlation to the type of family a person came from. A degree was therefore correlated with development that traditionally comes from the family. Thus, a degree held some employment value not for skills or knowledge obtained in college but as a proxy for other forms of development.

High schools encouraged students to prepare for college. The college path grew in social esteem while "technical" and "vocational" schools were viewed as the fallback path for those students who could not qualify for college.

For our discussion, we can skip many intervening details and look at current reality. As the demand for college increased and as the government subsidy for college cost increased, the price of a college degree escalated, far exceeding the average inflation rate over recent decades. Colleges responded to the demand and to government subsidy in two major ways. First, they created new degree programs and, when necessary, lowered admission standards. Second, they built new facilities to provide amenities and services to attract students. All of this activity and spending was driven by the idea that what mattered was the college degree. Often, little thought was given to whether the economy needed the schooling that was being offered or whether the students would have been better off with different preparation.

What was previously discernible but ignored the 2008 financial crisis made unavoidably clear. A college degree did not guarantee employment, let alone the type of job the student expected. However, this evidence did not cause a reevaluation of AHS. Rather, even more emphasis was placed on a college education. As one measure of this emphasis, student loan debt grew from $700 billion dollars in 2008 to $1.6 trillion in 2021. In spite of this huge growth in debt and in the number of people with at least some college training, employers today struggle to find employees with the right types of training. Ironically, while there is a surplus of people with college schooling who cannot find employment to their satisfaction, employers are struggling to fill positions that require skills not acquired in college, many paying more than jobs requiring a college degree.

Because of the misguided preference for college training, society is paying a high price. Many people, recent high school graduates as well as those who have been in the workforce for years, spent time and money for training they thought would lead to better employment opportunities. Some incurred debt that will burden them for many years. Society as a whole paid a price because the productive possibilities of people were not developed wisely. The economy needs skills that are now in short supply. Furthermore, at the time of this writing, some politicians are proposing that student debt be forgiven, which means that citizens who had no part in the bad decisions will pay off the debt.

Solution Framework

The first step in addressing a problem is to properly understand and frame the problem. Common ways of framing the problem look at objective outcomes such as many students graduating high school with the reading, writing, and math skills of a typical fifth grader. Or the problem is characterized by noting that the scores on standardized tests show American students well behind other countries. When the problem is understood in those ways, the natural solution is to attempt to improve basic skills and test scores by technical adjustments within schools. A great deal of time and money have been invested over decades trying to solve the problem framed in those ways. Today, there is little evidence of success, not because of some technical or procedural deficiency in the efforts but because the problem was improperly understood and framed.

How should the problem be framed? Begin with the real objective, which is not to improve basic skills by 10 percent or to move up a few spots in the international ranking but rather to prepare the next generation to be good citizens—productive, self-sustaining, and possessing the knowledge and character required of a citizen.

At the broadest level, we can frame the problem by saying that our preparation milieu is inadequate to prepare the next generation of citizens. Specific observations such as deficiency in basic skills, poor performance on standardized tests, inability to find and hold jobs, objections to structure and authority, and so on, are problematic, but they can't be fixed directly. The preparation milieu can only be made adequate by working from the most basic causes. That is what we will now explore for the purpose of sketching a solution framework.

This task of changing the preparation milieu is of first importance. Society will disintegrate if future generations are not prepared to assume the responsibilities of citizenship. One element of disintegration is taking center stage in the political debates at the time of this writing: the set of circumstances given the name *inequality*. Because of its importance, we have discussed this concept multiple times up to this point. That set of circumstances is primarily a result of our current preparation milieu. Today, those circumstances are more commonly blamed on the rulership structure or the economic structure. Those structures are not the primary causes for inequality.

If we want to improve the set of circumstances named inequality, we must improve the preparation milieu, which is primarily rooted in the social structure.

Our culture, our worldview, places a high value on fairness. A proper understanding of fairness is therefore an essential part of the development of a citizen. "Life is unfair" is often said because it is true. A person has no control over the family and community into which they are born. A person has no control over their genetic makeup or their prenatal and childhood environments. A person has no control over whether their natural abilities and interests align with what produces financial success. We want to "fix" those problems out of a sense of fairness, but what can society really do about them?

We know that treating undesirable symptoms as if they were the fundamental problems and then trying to fix them does not work. As a society, we have spent decades trying to address the problems of poverty and especially the disadvantages children in poverty experience. However, much of our effort and most of our money has been directed at mitigating symptoms rather than addressing fundamental causes. The result was socializing the costs, postponing real solutions, and making the true causes more difficult to change. Now reality has caught up with us. The results for the less fortunate members of society are getting worse, and we can no longer afford what it costs to mitigate and postpone.

We also know that society cannot remove differences in outcomes. The inevitable consequence of human nature and of how the world works is that there will always be differences. Attempts to make the outcomes of education equal will harm individuals and therefore harm society. Furthermore, it will reduce freedom and human dignity. Our focus must be on the causes of unfairness that result from the workings of society—that is, from structures of society.

Fortunately, society can make a difference; we can influence some of what the individual child has no control over. To do so requires a willingness to work on real causes, which in turn requires reframing the problem and being willing to take a longer view. The payoff will be better lives for all citizens.

The most important part of the picture that needs change is also the most difficult. It is to improve the quality of our families. There is no better predictor of the likelihood that a child will develop into a good citizen and have a successful life than the quality of the family in which they are raised. A society will always have families that do not function well and others that function superbly. For many decades, however, our trend has been toward growing numbers of families with increasing levels of dysfunction. In particular, a growing number of families are so dysfunctional that children have very little chance of good preparation for adulthood. No solution to the preparation of citizens, including that of schooling, will be successful when large numbers of children are growing up in highly dysfunctional families.

Up to this point, and because this chapter is about "education," we divided the subject into K-12 and AHS. To work on a solution framework, we need a broader division to cover from birth (including prenatal stage) to age 18, B-18. What happens from the prenatal period until kindergarten heavily influences how well a child will do in K-12. What happens in the K-12 years heavily influences AHS.

To emphasize a point, I will make an overly sharp distinction. I suggest that B-18 is properly a social concern, one that belongs inherently to all of society because the future of society depends on it. All citizens have a vested interest and therefore should invest in that phase of development. In contrast, I suggest that AHS belongs in the economic domain and is more a matter of personal responsibility than of social responsibility.

Although the pre-kindergarten stage of development is critical, it is outside the scope of this chapter. We therefore return our attention to formal schooling, with emphasis on K-12 because of its centrality to society.

In the past 40 years, we've seen heroic efforts from many teachers, well-intentioned policies and programs have been implemented, and we've roughly doubled inflation-adjusted spending on a per student basis. Yet students with a high school diploma are no better prepared as citizens than they were before that effort and expense. On average, in fact, they may be less prepared. When, after decades of effort and of increasing regulations and expenditure, the results are still trending down, we must ask why. What feedback is missing or distorted? Why has citizen voting (of all types) not brought improvements? What must change so solutions are possible?

In any such analysis a good place to start is to look at power, money, and worldview (what do segments of society believe and value about the issue?). In this case, a quick review of some facts reveals why the average citizen cannot act like an owner or ruler. It is difficult to hold people accountable and to effect change via political and economic voting.

Government has monopoly control over public education. All funding, regulation, and certification are controlled by local, state, and federal government. In addition to monopoly control by government, public schools are in practice a monopoly for all but those who can afford to pay both taxes for public schools and tuition for private schools. That is, for most families, the only school option available is the local public school.

While it varies by state, funding for public schools accounts for roughly one-third of local and state government expenditures. Estimates vary much, but total K-12 spending in the United States starts on the low end around $800 billion per year. Present and incurred expenses are likely significantly higher. In any event, a lot of money is directed toward education, and where there is a lot of money there are usually multiple parties with a vested interest in retaining all of the current structure. All of this money comes from a complicated tax and distribution structure with deep roots in social and economic substructures.

Local and state governments employ over 6.5 million people in public education, a number that is about one half of total local and state government employment. These employees represent a large and effective (political) voting bloc. About half of public school employees are teachers, many of whom belong to unions that may well have powerful political influence. To be clear, not all of those 6.5 million people, nor all of the teachers, are certain that public school as it is configured today is the best solution for students.

More than vested interests keep the current system locked into place. Public school has always been important in American life. It is how we do things. Public schools used to augment the passing on of culture and character to the next generation. Today, with diverging ideas and values related to culture and character, public schools are often the focus of contention in this regard. As a direct result of that conflict, some groups within society want to win the battle of what culture and character (beliefs and values) will be taught and then use the public school monopoly to propagate their views. Finally, many people believe that "education" is a solution to multiple social and economic problems. Because government controls public schools, it wants to retain that control in hopes that they can yet find a solution to those social and economic problems.

Using those facts, we can explain why nothing has changed for many decades by looking at the distorted feedback signals and the potential improvements which have been blocked. For this discussion, we will look at political and economic voting only because they are more significant than social voting in this case. Part of our explanation is based upon scenarios for two families.

A technical note: much of the local funding for schools comes from property taxes. Property tax rates vary by school district and are determined by votes of the citizens in the district. The higher the tax rate and the higher the value of properties in the district, the higher the revenue for the schools.

Consider first a family with some excess financial capacity. This does not mean that they are wealthy, only that they have more income than is required for a reasonable standard of living. Such a family has at least two options. They could choose to live in a lower tax district and use the tax savings together with other income to send their children to a private school. The other option is to move to a school district with higher tax rates and higher-priced homes and then have their children attend public schools. In this option, the family will have a better-than-average public school experience for two reasons. The most important is that such districts tend to have a lower percentage of families whose children will need school-based social services and surrogate parenting. Secondly, that district will likely attract better teachers because they can pay more and because the working environment is more attractive.

Those better-off families may make such a choice simply to have their children attend a school in which they can achieve better schooling. Not only do these better schools have good teachers and a good learning environment, they often offer a broader range of learning opportunities than do struggling schools. A second reason, and one growing in importance, is driven by the diverging values within society and the aims of different groups who want to control what culture and character are taught in schools. Private schools options let the family decide which school teaches the beliefs and values important to the family. Even among public schools—though they are constrained by regulations—some will more closely align with what the parents desire.

Our second family is toward the other end of the socioeconomic spectrum. It is a good month when they can pay their bills for housing, food, and basic necessities. The children qualify for subsidized school meal programs. Unfortunately, they live in a district in which many families are struggling not just economically but are also not providing a quality home environment. While our second family wants their children to get an education and to have a better life, they know that the public school in their district—where their children must attend—spends much of every day trying to maintain order and provide social and parental services. But this family has no options.

On first analysis, we might say that the first family had economic voting power while the second did not. However, more careful consideration shows that the first family had more options because of greater financial resources. For example, if the first family chose the option of living in a lower-tax district, they are paying property taxes to support the public schools while at the same time paying to support a private school. Contrast this to a pure economic vote when true choices are available. If a family pays a little more to purchase products from Company A because it treats its employees better than Company B, the family has made a clear economic vote. It is not supporting both companies. However, that is not the case for the family that chooses private schooling; they must support both public and private systems.

Moving from economic voting to political voting, why has the latter not provided a solution? The answer has several components. For many decades, it was commonly believed that if more regulations and programs were put in place and if more money was spent, the existing system could work for all citizens. That approach has failed, and growing numbers of citizens and leaders are acknowledging the fact, so much so that in recent elections, several states voted to favor more school choice.

A second part of the answer is that those with a vested interest in maintaining the current system, whether for reasons of power, money, or worldview, are more organized and more successful in generating political opposition to fundamental changes.

The third part of the answer is that the problem is legitimately difficult. It is complex. Even setting aside objections from vested interests, proposals for new approaches are met with reasonable questions about fairness and the mechanics of implementation. The problems sometimes seem unsolvable.

Finally, the problem of K-12 schooling is not urgent for all Americans. Those with the largest potential political and economic clout are often not personally impacted. They are more likely to live in locations with good schools and have the finances to get their kids into them. A large middle group of families who can't afford the best schools but are also not in the worst situations are satisfied enough with their local public school that it is not a pressing issue for them. Those families most in need are the ones lacking most in knowledge and influence. In many cases, it is fair to say they are lost.

Thus, we face a social problem of tremendous importance yet which so far has been intractable. What must happen for the problem to become important and urgent enough to demand a solution? When we are ready to solve the problem, what concepts, in addition to the above, can guide solutions?

Because it is a critical point, let's remember that the problems in our preparation milieu, including K-12 specifically, cannot be solved until we address even broader problems within society—the most important of which is the quality of our families. Those broader problems will be taken up in the next part of the book. The problems do not have to be addressed sequentially. Those issues of broader society and the issues associated with schooling and other specific aspects of the preparation milieu can be and should be addressed in parallel.

In order for the problems in our preparation milieu, and specifically K-12, to become important and urgent enough for action, several things must happen. First, and most importantly, a majority of Americans must think about the problem through the lens of "self-interest properly understood." Societies fail when in each new generation a growing number of children are not adequately prepared to be citizens of a free society. This condition exists now—and not only for those in the unfortunate segments of society. In addition, the poor quality of many of our K-12 institutions is a primary cause of inequality and unfairness. As seen in recent elections in the United States and elsewhere in the world, what is called a "populist" vote has grown. This is often a sign of serious problems developing in a society.

When the time comes that enough Americans are sufficiently motivated to solve the problem, we face an admittedly difficult problem that won't be solved by simple adjustments to the current system. I suggest the following points should inform our solutions.

Parents, regardless of economic resources, need school choice. Of the several issues to be addressed, two will be foundational: 1) monopoly control of schooling by government must end, and 2) the funding structure for K-12 schooling must be reworked.

The significance of a high school diploma needs to be redefined. Currently, a diploma may represent that the holder has been very well prepared as a citizen and for whatever comes later. On the other hand, a diploma may simply mean that a person has sat in a classroom for 12 years but is not prepared as a citizen and is functionally illiterate. No one benefits from this confusion. Possible details of what the redefinition of K-12 might be are beyond the scope of this book. But it is an essential task.

Above, I characterized K-12 as a broad social issue and one for which society as a whole has responsibility. It poses a difficult problem as outlined above. Likewise, AHS was characterized as an economic issue and more of a personal responsibility. When we look forward to a properly functioning K-12 system, much of the AHS problem goes away, and what remains can easily be addressed.

Conceptually, we have only one idea to overcome. At present, college is preferred socially and economically. "College for everyone" is often put forward as a solution for inequality and a host of other social issues. The data are now rapidly accumulating to show that it is a bad idea. Interestingly, some companies have begun dropping the requirement of a college degree and are instead offering their own in-house training in order to get qualified workers. As noted earlier, this strong preference for a college degree would not have developed were it not for the distortion caused by government subsidies.

Government support for colleges includes direct budgetary support, student financing, and social encouragement. Such support dwarfs that provided to all other AHS options combined. These pro-college policies are maintained even though they contribute to perhaps the most pressing social issue of our time: inequality. Much of the pro-college funding came through debt—which is yet to be paid.

If society decides it is worthwhile to subsidize AHS, it would do more to help society and to minimize economic differences if all AHS paths were supported proportionally.

While I'm not proposing this as policy, a thought experiment can help clarify our understanding of AHS. Imagine the government announced that beginning immediately all forms of financial subsidy to colleges and other AHS paths (including subsidized loans) would be reduced over the following three years, at which point the costs for any AHS training would be the personal responsibility of the individual. A rapid adjustment would take place such that the AHS structure would align with what the economy needed.

A secondary consequence of the thought experiment would be an adjustment of what society esteems. As individuals turned their attention and effort to learning how to do what society needs, esteem would go to those who successfully met those needs. What is honorable is a citizen who is self-supporting by meeting the needs of other citizens, completely independent of any piece of certifying paper.

Summary

For many decades, we've looked to "education" as the primary solution to social and economic problems. However, as discussed throughout this book, the many changes and distortions that came about in the twentieth century caused us to lose a proper understanding of what is required for the development of a citizen. A combination of huge social changes and huge government-financial distortion, caused by our monetary and financial structure, created a schooling structure that increasingly worked well for a shrinking percentage of citizens. Today, our schooling structure is fueling inequality rather than working toward fairness. This fact is becoming more clear to more people, and thus we can be hopeful that reform is coming soon.

ECONOMIC SYSTEM

"The only way that has ever been discovered to have a lot of people cooperate together voluntarily is through the free market. And that's why it's so essential to preserving individual freedom."
Milton Friedman

"It is a singular fact that this steadily increasing prosperity, far from tranquilizing the population, everywhere promoted a spirit of unrest..."
Alexis de Tocqueville

Our time calls for a new analysis of our economic system. Many criticisms are directed at it as the most important cause of economic inequality. Our economic system is criticized for things for which it is not to blame and is absolved of criticism where it is deserved. A proper understanding is urgent because the intensity of criticism has reached the level at which an avowed socialist was a strong contender in the 2020 presidential election, something unthinkable a decade earlier. A proper understanding is important because we risk making changes that will increase inequality rather than decrease it, hurt rather than help those at the bottom, and reduce overall material prosperity.

Therefore, before we look at what could be changed in our economic system to reduce unnecessary differences we will first define terms and review what has been learned by economic experiments around the world over the past 70 years.

Capitalism has been increasingly criticized. In the last presidential debate, the issue was framed as capitalism versus socialism. These words are poorly defined and are used by different people to mean widely different things. For those who are harshly critical of our current economic system, *capitalism* often means simply "the results we are now getting" while *socialism* means "the results we want." For those who defend our current economic system, capitalism often means (1) our current structure of production, and (2) the material prosperity our current system produces, whereas socialism means government control of private property. Such loose definitions are dangerous.

Critics of our current system see capitalism as free markets taken too far. For extreme critics, the solution is to replace capitalism with socialism, by which they mean some system that retains prosperity but is more fair. Supporters of our current system often see capitalism as distorted through overregulation by the government and see the solution as less regulation along with increased personal responsibility.

To avoid the confused meanings and connotations, this chapter will most often use *economic system* and will use *capitalism* and *socialism* only when necessary for distinction. When used, the latter terms will have the following meanings based upon the essential principle in each system. *Capitalism* will refer to private property and economic freedom. *Socialism* will mean government control of the economy, which entails reduced economic freedom and government control, if not formal ownership, of property.

No economic system is perfect. Each will bring challenges that must be addressed by society. The most famous and harshest critic of capitalism, Karl Marx, acknowledged that capitalism produced more material prosperity than socialism. He advocated communism—knowing that material prosperity would be reduced—because he thought it would produce a happier society. Marx saw socialism as a step toward communism.

Marx misunderstood human nature and economic principles. The past 100 years have shown that communist regimes result in widespread death, poverty, and suffering. Countries that are socialist more than communist sometimes avoid massive deaths but still bring poverty and suffering.

When the Soviet Union collapsed around 1990, the free market system (capitalism) was widely proclaimed as the victor and as the future. In recent years, however, the world has seen a sharp reversal of those assessments. Capitalism is now under attack. People around the world, including many in the United States, blamed American-style capitalism for the financial crisis of 2008. More recently, a growing number of Americans blame our economic system for circumstances and opportunities judged as unfair, all of which are lumped into the single term *inequality* in the public debate.

Venezuela once again provides a vivid example of the harm that comes from poorly understood decisions regarding the economic system of a society. As we saw earlier in the book, the people of Venezuela are suffering because they elected a leader who supported socialism. How could this have happened? The people of Venezuela were free and had free access to information. They had many examples over previous decades of other countries in the region that had suffered under socialist-type governments. They had the example of the collapse of the Soviet Union, after which it became clear to the world the extent to which communism had failed. They had the examples of Europe and the United States to show that freedom and prosperity come from governments that are not on the socialist-communist path. In spite of all of this, they freely voted for socialism.

As American citizens we should not assume that somehow we are different, that we can solve our problems by radical changes to our economic system. We are not different; we are subject to the same economic principles. Yet some Americans are wondering if this might be the answer. That is why proper understanding of economic systems is urgent and important.

Why do many citizens think first of making changes to the economic system, whether they be relatively small changes in policy and regulation or more dramatic changes such as moving from a free economy to a government-controlled economy? One reason is that almost every problem today appears to be an economic problem, and we are conditioned to believe that economic problems can be solved by the government. We must change that understanding.

The previous chapter, while titled "Education," was about the broad preparation of young people to become citizens. It discussed the concept of "preparation milieu," which encompasses much more than schooling. It includes the quality of families, the role of community, and the influence of media. The issues discussed in that chapter come before and are more fundamental than those directly connected to our economic system. No changes within our economic system can compensate for the hard work of forming a citizen.

Our discussion in this chapter assumes that the problems presented in the previous chapter will be seen as a higher priority and will be addressed in parallel with changes to the economic system.

In order to think clearly about our economic system, we must first dispel a few common beliefs, some of which have become so ingrained they are assumed to be economic principles. Our economic system is not completely free market. That is, our problem is not one of too much economic freedom. Much of economic activity is heavily regulated by the government and is influenced by a complicated tax code. Even more significant is the government-controlled structure of money and finance as discussed in an earlier chapter. It is that structure that drives recessions. It is not true, as commonly believed, that recessions are a normal part of "capitalism." The 2008 recession, widely judged as the worst since the Great Depression, had its origin completely within the monetary and financial structure, and much of that activity was motivated and made possible by government regulations put in place over the previous two decades.

Another misconception that plays out in every election is the idea that government can create jobs and make the economy grow. It cannot. The government of one country can try to attract business from another country to itself. One state can try to attract business to locate within it rather than in another. Government, through the monetary system or debt, may artificially and temporarily stimulate economic activity but the economy will later adjust through recession. Government can, and sometimes should, control and regulate certain economic activity, but that will always result in reduced economic output in exchange for some other social good. In general, government cannot create economic productivity. When citizens via political votes encourage or allow such government attempts, some price will be paid. One part of the country may pay for another part. One industry may pay for others. Taxes may go up, inflation may rise. But the net effect for the country as a whole must be less than zero.

Many citizens believe that the causes of unfair inequality are easily identifiable issues such as immigration, globalization, technology, or greed. Under stress, it is human nature to look for something that can be identified, blamed, and attacked. Although each of the issues in that short list might come into play in some ways, their effect is relatively minor.

Attempts to fix our social problems by isolating "capitalism" and treating it as a separate thing that can be "fixed" falls into a common trap: the idea that we can fix one problem at a time. Properly understood, our economic system is inextricably integrated with all other aspects of society. Just as we can't fix our preparation milieu by simply addressing schooling, we can't fix economic problems by simply addressing "capitalism."

Our important and urgent social problem now is to properly understand our economic system and its interactions with other social structures and conditions so we can find solutions that retain our freedoms and material prosperity while minimizing the problems of inequality. With the background established in the first part of the chapter, we now turn to understanding how the economic system contributes to conditions sometimes judged as unfair and what we as citizens can change to bring improvement.

Because we want to keep our freedoms and material prosperity and because we want opportunities for future generations, we must make all of our decisions in light of the principles upon which our economic system is built. The primary principles are private property and economic freedom. A natural outcome of those principles is that all economic activity is coordinated by prices. That is, consumers signal what goods and services they want by the actual purchases they make. A business can only continue to function if it makes a profit, and it can only make a profit if it provides what consumers want at a price they are willing to pay. This is the basis of the incredibly powerful economic voting of citizens.

An economic law that holds true under any economic system whether free or despotic is that consumption must be preceded by production. Bread must be produced before it can be eaten. This might seem so obvious that it need not be mentioned let alone emphasized. However, under a monetary system in which money can be created out of nothing, it is easy to lose sight of this most fundamental economic law. The mistake is thinking that money possesses its own productive power rather than recognizing that money simply facilitates production and consumption. We fall into that error more than we realize, especially with regard to government spending.

When pricing signals are distorted or when society operates as if consumption can precede production, the economy will suffer in some way. Almost always, that suffering works to the disadvantage of those who are already in the most economically disadvantaged position. Therefore, when looking for ways in which the economic system increases inequality, we will look to where these principles are compromised: government action.

Government action is shorthand for a group of elected leaders responding to the political, social, and economic voting of citizens. This is good news because it means that citizens can vote to change those aspects of our economic system that harm other citizens. Only two things are required. First, citizens must have a proper understanding of their voting and its consequences. This is part of retaking our rulership role, of truly accepting our responsibilities as owners. Second, we must be willing to cast those votes even if in the short-term, and in specific details, our votes do not appear to be to our personal advantage. That is, we must keep the perspective of "self-interest properly understood."

Government acts through four primary mechanisms: (1) taxes, (2) spending, (3) laws and regulations that prescribe, proscribe, and encourage behavior, and (4) monetary policy. While we could list hundreds, probably thousands, of specific examples, such a list would not serve the purposes of this book. Rather, we will look at the underlying concepts in play in all of those areas.

An overarching perspective will help our understanding. First, we recall that all government action reduces the freedom of some group or favors one group over another. The natural tendency is for citizens to petition "government" to do something that favors the groups to which they belong. As Frederic Bastiat said, "Government is the great fiction through which everybody endeavors to live at the expense of everybody else." As citizen-rulers, if we operate from that mindset, we will bring ruin to our society. Instead, with each political or economic vote we cast, we can imagine ourselves in the position of all other affected citizens and ask this operative question, "If I were in their position, how would I cast my political, social, or economic vote?"

We need government, of course, yet the actions of government necessarily distort the pricing structure within the economic system. Citizens have the responsibility of deciding if a particular government action will bring enough benefit to offset its cost, not only the immediate cost of taxes or debt but also the cost associated with altering the price signals and therefore altering the incentives within society. As discussed in previous chapters, making such assessments has been difficult for the past 70 years because unique circumstances together with new monetary systems made it difficult to see and understand real costs and, even when they were seen, made it easy to push back the payment of those costs onto later generations.

Sometimes, government policies intended to help a situation have the opposite effect. In the 1960s, the government declared a "war on poverty" aimed at helping those at the bottom of the socio-economic spectrum. In one way or the other, such policies have continued since then. However, not only did those policies fail to reduce inequality, they created one of the biggest structural supports for inequality. The programs reduced personal responsibility and incentive to work. Each successive generation growing up under those policies has received less training to be a productive citizen and is therefore unprepared for employment.

In many places throughout this book we've noted the impact of our monetary system, that is, of our monetary and financial structure. It is the enabler of almost all of the substructures within our economic system that contribute to economic inequality. Because its influence has been discussed in other chapters, here we will simply make a few summary statements. It causes inflation, which hurts the poor more than other segments of society. It encourages a structure of production that favors capital expenditure over labor. It allows the funding of government policies that favor those who are better off and hurt those at the bottom. It concentrates power in the federal government, in the financial industry, and in the largest corporations, all of which work to the harm of those lowest on the economic ladder.

It is not popular to discuss the structural effects we just reviewed. They are politically and functionally difficult to change. It is easier to think that unfair differences in the economy are caused by things more easily identified and blamed, examples of which were discussed earlier in the chapter. Only if we are willing to make changes in the fundamental structural effects can we hope to improve what might be wrong in those things that are easily identified and commonly blamed.

All of the structural bases for inequality just reviewed depend on the votes of citizens, and in this case, the most important votes are political. However, our economic votes also support structures that work to the disadvantage of lower income citizens.

This can most easily be explained by an example. Some companies are criticized for paying low wages and offering minimal if any benefits. Yet, often the same citizens who criticize those companies also shop there to take advantage of the low prices. It is, of course, the economic votes of citizens that determine how companies operate. It is unlikely a competitor would enter the market and hope to make a profit by paying wages 25 percent higher than the industry average because it is clear from past experience that consumers will not pay a substantially higher price for something simply to support higher wages for workers.

Summary

When the social issue of inequality is discussed, the focus usually turns first to our economic system because the most obvious manifestations of inequality are economic. The most fundamental drivers of inequality, however, are in our social structures as discussed in the previous chapter. Only if we accept that fact and are willing to work on those areas can we make real progress within our economic system.

In our public debate, *capitalism* and *socialism* are not helpful terms because neither are well-defined. Stated simplistically, *capitalism* often means simply what we have now, and *socialism* means something better than what we have now. Nowhere is the careless use of words more common and more dangerous than in the economic domain. That is why in this chapter those words have been largely avoided in preference of talking about principles, structures, and specific issues.

Any economic system presents challenges to society. There is no perfect system, and it is critically important to recognize that reality. Attempts at economic utopia, for example, the theory of Karl Marx, always result in great suffering.

Economic systems based, however imperfectly, on private property and economic freedom have raised hundreds of millions of people (perhaps billions) out of abject poverty and have raised life expectancy significantly. No economic system in the history of the world has done as well. No other economic system offers more possibility for those who are poor to improve their situation. Therefore, our task is to retain those principles while working on social and economic structures that create unfairness in society.

In our political system, when we talk about economic problems, it is easier to focus on things that are easy to identify and blame than it is to think carefully about principles and structures. However, the latter approach must be pursued because the former approach will solve nothing and is more likely to create additional problems.

Finally, a reminder that inequality is a fact of life. Every economic system produces inequality; only the nature of the inequality distribution changes. The best we can do is change those things that unfairly favor one group over another. Fortunately, in a democracy, the citizens by their political, economic, and social votes have the power to make those changes.

Part IV

GOING FORWARD

"We all want progress, but if you're on the wrong road, progress means doing an about-turn and walking back to the right road; in that case, the man who turns back soonest is the most progressive."
C. S. Lewis

"In the moment of crisis, the wise build bridges, and the foolish build dams."
Nigerian proverb

DON'T JUST "DO SOMETHING"

"The whole problem with the world is that fools and fanatics are always so certain of themselves, and wiser people so full of doubts."
Bertrand Russell

". . . the learned give up the evidence of their senses to preserve the coherence of the ideas of their imagination."
Adam Smith

"Do something" is an attitude that has served America well for most of 250 years. It is still a useful perspective as long as we have proper understanding. However, as we've discussed in many places throughout this book, having a proper understanding has become increasingly difficult in the past 70 years. Our *capacity* to do things outran our understanding of what *should* be done. The implicit bargain between the citizenry and a governing elite was based on the premise that government could manage society. People on both sides of that bargain worked on the assumption that "doing something" would indeed result in a well-managed society and would provide solutions to problems.

Up to this point in the book, we've looked at why that bargain developed, on what assumptions it was based, and why it failed. Indeed, the worldview and circumstances in place following World War II together with human nature made failure almost unavoidable.

Our generation, our time, is now coming to terms with the distortions and postponed costs of the many isolated "do something" policies. Some citizens are responding to what they see as a stream of present crises and others to what they see as an impending crisis of huge consequence. A majority of citizens and perhaps an even larger majority of those in positions of power still believe (hope) that targeted "do something" actions will produce solutions if only we find the right "something" to do.

When we pursue "do something" solutions to a specific problem in isolation, the common approach is to treat the symptoms rather than the cause. That is, our natural tendency for quick solutions encourages government officials to mitigate or mask symptoms. Decades of "doing something" has increased the cost and size of government, concentrated more power within government, reduced freedoms, and more often than not made the targeted problem worse. Thus, we must pursue the alternative approach.

In the first three parts of this book, we've not only shown why the above approach failed but also laid the foundations for developing effective solutions. In this part of the book, we will look in more concrete detail at how citizens can work toward real solutions going forward. We certainly need to act, but action must be based on proper understanding.

Our situation calls for urgent action but not urgent solutions. What is urgent is a changed mindset, proper understanding, and an intense desire to generate viable solutions for the fundamental causes of our problems. This is exactly opposite of the last 50-plus years. We must begin at the root of the problem rather than the symptomatic end, and we must consider the broad forces in society that worked together to create problems rather than assuming there is a single, fixable cause to a problem. This approach, in addition to the obvious advantage of producing viable solutions, has other advantages, including increased freedoms, reduced costs, and decreased concentrations of power.

First, we must truly accept that our social problems are the results of the votes of citizens. In our country, we enjoy freedom of voting: politically, economically, and socially. The military does not "encourage" how we vote. With that acceptance, it is a small step to understand that we the citizens must resume our role as rulers. In the chapter, "Thinking Like a Ruler," we used the analogy of owners who eventually realized that their company was being run poorly because they, the owners, had given too much authority and responsibility to the managers of the company. The fix was to assume the proper role of owner. We as citizen-rulers must do the same.

As citizen-rulers assuming a more responsible role in society, we have a great deal to learn and new skills to develop, just as the newly responsible owners of the business faced. However, citizen-rulers must learn things different in kind and difficulty than what was faced by the business owners. Furthermore, citizen-rulers have to unlearn a number of things that have become "common knowledge" over decades. This book is intended as a start toward such proper understanding, including the concept of "self-interest properly understood," which is constantly in play in society. Each citizen must consider both their own benefit and that of society as a whole.

Let's assume that a group of citizens has accepted this new role and has invested time in developing proper understanding, part of which will include the principles and analyses from previous parts of this book. Those citizens bring an immediate advantage to society. Because they understand that their votes shape society, they will be more intentional about each decision they make. Setting aside explicitly political votes (ballot box), here are examples of economic and social voting. Here, the focus is on the voting aspect of the decision, not on the technical superiority of one product versus another.

Each product (or service) they purchase casts multiple small votes. The purchase itself signals that the thing purchased is valued. It encourages more production of that product. The purchase informs that industry whether customers are looking for low price or high quality, low service or high service, and so on. Purchasing the product from a particular company is a vote for how that company conducts business, how it treats employees, and what values it promulgates.

In addition, some purchases cast a significant social or political vote. Some companies are in the business of providing and shaping information. Purchasing or using the products (or services) provided by those companies is a vote supporting their political and social views, their philosophy of how information should be controlled, and the direct political influence they wield. Some of the most influential companies offer their products or services ostensibly for free. But nothing is free. The consumer is making a purchase whether or not it is clear or explicit. Thus, "using" casts the same vote as an explicit purchase.

Many comments we make in conversation or post on social media or communicate in our professional roles are social votes. Our comments convey what we value, how we think things should work, our opinion of those we disagree with, and so on. Our comments affect others, and the comments of others affect us.

For many of our daily actions, as illustrated above, we are adequately guided by always remembering that as a citizen-ruler, every vote of every type matters. We can make use of the principles and analyses presented earlier in this book to guide our thinking. However, in other cases, we face a challenge because we live in a world that is complexly organized and highly specialized. No single person can obtain all of the information they need to make an informed decision. To make the situation more difficult, the degree of complexity and specialization has increased rapidly at the same time that trusted sources of guidance and authority have been increasingly discredited.

To illustrate, in 1950, the public had a relatively high level of trust in the government, the church, and science. Today, for various reasons, the level of trust in these institutions is exceptionally low. Furthermore, in 1950 an individual could have a better grasp of a wider range of issues of public concern. Today, a person may need to dedicate most of their career to a single aspect of a single subject. Finally, in the past couple of decades our society has become extremely politicized. For reasons discussed earlier in the book, different groups of citizens are fighting intensely for the control of government. Each competing party is so confident that it alone is right and the struggle is so intense that many individuals and organizations believe winning at any cost is justified. Standards of ethics and integrity that once were taken for granted are now too easily abandoned.

We can hope—and this book is based on the hope—that trust, integrity, and ethics will be restored through the actions (voting) of citizens, but that will take time. How, in the meantime, do citizen-rulers obtain the information and expertise required for good voting? Government agencies that used to be one step removed from direct political influence have in recent years become highly politicized. Individuals and organizations who once operated in a trustworthy manner under the mantle of science have also been compromised by ideology and the desire for power and money. The same assessment applies to most sources of news and communication. There are exceptions in each area, of course, but it is difficult to identify them. Thus, something new is needed, a new primary source of information, expertise, and advice. By "primary" I mean a source that has earned a high level of trust by being truthful, by honoring facts, by working with fundamental principles, and by doing competent analyses.

Fortunately, the solution to the immediate problem also offers a long-term counterweight to those who are in pursuit of power and money and who are willing to sacrifice integrity, ethics, and trust. Our society needs a parallel network of trusted information, expertise, and advice. It is beyond the scope of this book to attempt to explore in detail what that might look like, but we do know some parameters. Government agencies and all entities that receive federal funding or are heavily regulated by government would most likely not be a primary source. That removes many organizations from the primary level. Without prejudice, and for illustration, a few examples are research universities, some research labs, education, banking, and the defense industry.

Some of those entities that cannot meet the standards of a primary source may still be useful secondary sources. "Secondary" means that the entities may provide useful raw data or useful analyses as long as their conflict of interest is taken into account.

A clarification is needed for the above paragraphs. Within the agencies and entities listed above as secondary sources, there are dedicated people who try to be a nonpolitical provider of information and expertise. However, their contribution is restricted and modified by those at the top of those organizations. Citizen-rulers hope and work for the time when the contribution of those who want to serve society with integrity is freely available and assessable.

Companies in the communications business, both those who primarily produce content and those who provide platforms, could also be secondary sources. Some companies in this category might earn status as a trusted source, but it is difficult.

Entities that corrupt data, are deceitful in communications, censor communications, or shut down dissenting voices fall into the untrusted category. They are not useful for citizen-rulers. Note, simply because an organization has a biased viewpoint does not mean it is a source to be avoided. A biased view can be useful if the source is honest and competent.

Most primary sources would likely be nonprofit organizations that receive no government funding and do not support political parties or candidates. Another primary source could be individual thinkers and researchers who function outside of any formal entity and who also receive no government funding. A free society needs such organizations and individuals who are willing to serve society by investing their time and talent for the greater long-term good. Citizens of course must assess each organization and individual with regard to fundamental principles, worldview, and honest analysis.

The good news is that some of the components needed for such a trusted network of primary sources already exist and are playing a valuable role in society. We don't have to build from scratch. What is needed is a growing number of citizens willing to engage with the organizations and individuals who may qualify as primary sources. This engagement will be an investment of time and money.

The development of new primary sources of information, expertise, and advice will bring several advantages to society. Citizens will have more responsive and productive sources from which to receive information and in turn to shape the sources themselves. Those organizations and individuals who by the informal votes of citizens establish themselves as primary sources will have elevated influence. They will also have elevated accountability. Those who currently hold power in government and otherwise, those who recently have been called the "ruling elite," will respond to this effort by citizens. Their first response may be to restrict information and attempt to stop the development of the new primary trusted network. But if citizens persevere, those in power will adjust, not wanting to be secondary.

While the development of a new primary source of information, expertise, and advice is necessary for citizen-rulers to regain control and initiate real reform, the effort will also provide a long-term benefit. All power needs checks and balances. Having a new primary source of information will serve as a check and balance against the traditional and formal sources, not least of which is government.

Realistically, many citizens will not have the time, willingness, or ability to engage significantly with a new network of trusted information, expertise, and advice. As long as a growing number of citizens do engage and do invest the effort, however, progress will be made. Those citizens who do not engage directly with these primary sources will exercise their citizen-ruler role in different ways. At a minimum, a large majority of citizens must commit to understanding fundamental principles. Citizens who do not invest time to study analyses from primary sources may still learn to rely on them for opinions. Furthermore, many citizens have the opportunity to personally engage with fellow citizens who do have the time, willingness, and ability to firmly grasp analyses of our current institutions.

As citizens begin moving in the directions outlined above, fewer and fewer citizens will be easily swayed by political promises and policies that are inconsistent with principles, based on poor or dishonest analyses, or that clearly violate the concept of "self-interest properly understood."

In the two following chapters, we will investigate two subjects which are significant causes of our social problems. The first deals with competing worldviews, the second with responsibility and feedback. For each of these areas, we will discuss specific things that citizen-rulers can do to bring about change.

Some of the necessary changes will require investment and perseverance over years. Some of what is required will impose more costs and effort on some citizens than on others. The final chapter of this part of the book discusses the idea of transitions, that is, how a society can move from one state to another in an orderly manner in ways that seem reasonable and fair.

COMPETING WORLDVIEWS

"A house divided against itself cannot stand."
Abraham Lincoln

"Everyone has some kind of philosophy, some general worldview, which to men of other views will seem mythological."
H. Richard Niebuhr

At the heart of our social problems, our frustration, and our political contention is competition among worldviews. More specifically, it is competition between major elements of our worldviews. If we are to solve our problems and move forward as a society, we must find ways to deal with this competition.

The most powerful element of our worldviews is our belief system, which for most of history went under the name *religion*. Belief systems are powerful enough to be the primary causes of a society's greatness or of its decline. Throughout history, those who have held competing worldviews have too often been willing to subdue, coerce, or abuse those who held conflicting views. Belief systems may be so strong that people will kill or die for them.

As we saw earlier in this book, we make a mistake if we assume that our world is being freed of belief systems—speaking of the West now— because the traditional religion of Christianity has lost much of its influence. The experiences of the last 120 years, including the struggles of our time and society, have proved conclusively that "anti-religious" belief systems generate passions and actions comparable with any "religion."

Our challenge is to figure out what we are going to do now that our citizens hold competing worldviews, the most important element of which is belief systems. The belief system of an individual may strongly influence the other two elements of a worldview we will consider here: economics and life in a free society. However, that relationship is not necessarily strong. It is quite possible that people with different, even competing, belief systems will nonetheless share similar understandings of how an economy should function or how life should be lived in a free society.

Our challenge is complicated by three other circumstances, all of which have been discussed previously. First, the concentration of power in the federal government encourages each group to aggressively pursue control of the government. Second, our multiple, specific social problems are not responding to solutions and are becoming more intense. Third, as discussed in the chapter "Social Structure," the influence of anomie is growing.

From these conditions flow three behaviors that must be reversed before we can make progress on learning how to be a society with competing worldviews. These behaviors are listed separately because they manifest that way in society, but all are aspects of freedom. First, free speech is increasingly suppressed. Second, some leaders in government and some non-government elites feel justified suppressing and distorting information for the purpose of shaping the thinking of citizens. A few go further and engage in outright deception.

Unfortunately, some ordinary citizens acquiesce to this behavior if it supports their beliefs. Third, and most damaging, some groups are willing to coerce others to act against their values and to censor dissenting views. Recent examples include people losing their jobs because of their speech or beliefs, and being forced to endorse behavior with which they disagree. Current topics that generate this response include climate control, pandemic management, and gay marriage. Coercion is the most urgent and dangerous of the three behaviors because it can quickly escalate conflict and endanger a working society.

What can be done?

The first step is for citizens to realize that our society is under serious threat. Business as usual won't continue forever. The first and most important task is to regain a proper understanding of freedom. Freedom does not mean that we are free from discomfort, economic challenges, or life's inherent risks. Freedom does not mean that we are free from facing facts or what makes us uncomfortable. From the beginnings of democratic thought more than 2,500 years ago, it was recognized that freedom could easily degrade into selfishness and license. True freedom means the right to live life in the pursuit of virtue, to be a productive citizen of society, and do to so without coercion.

The second step is acceptance of the reality that political cooperation among the major political parties is not going to be the short-term solution. The common call, made for the past 20 years, for "Washington to learn to work together" is not possible at present. As citizens, we must accept the uncomfortable truth that Washington is configured as it is because of our political, economic, and social voting over many decades. Ultimately, of course, we must have cooperative leadership, not only in Washington, but also in our state governments. However, that will happen only when citizens gain a proper understanding and decide to assume their responsibility as citizen-rulers.

On the political spectrum, a small percentage of citizens hold views on the extreme left and right. On either side of the line separating the left and the right is the vast majority of citizens who do not endorse the views of those on the extremes. In fact, a large majority of citizens on either side of the line share many common values, goals, and views of society.

Imagine an evening social event attended by an equal number of people on either side of the political dividing line who are closer to the middle than to the extremes. Assume each person in attendance agrees not to divulge on which side of the line they reside, not to speak explicitly of politics, but only visit among themselves to discuss values, what they want for their families and for society, and what their views of justice are. They would find a great deal in common. When the event was over and everyone was headed home they would think they had been in the company of good people who were much like themselves. They might wonder how the country could be so sharply divided.

So why does the political environment remain so polarized? The primary reason is because all special interest groups are determined to gain control of the one entity powerful enough to force others to do what they think should be done. In our present circumstances, the distribution of political views is such that the extremes on each side of the dividing line hold a disproportionate political vote that gives them enough influence to effectively stalemate our political system. But this only happens because the vast majority of citizens closer to the center line are afraid that if they "cross over" even slightly, the other extreme will gain more influence. That fear has merit given today's configuration.

Something new must happen. But what? Each side takes a risk if it compromises first. We cannot in one quick step dissolve the political stalemate nor restore trust. A progression is required. Fortunately, there are things citizen-rulers in the middle of the spectrum can do without turning power over to the "other side." All of these things depend upon each person taking the time required to look at each issue from the perspective of others.

Using that perspective, we will look at the three related behaviors noted above, which have to do with freedom and must be reversed. In addition to that perspective, we will also apply principles, the most important of which for this discussion deal with power: (1) once a power is taken or is granted, it is rare that it will later be relinquished; (2) once a power has been granted, it is usually expanded beyond its original intent and will have consequences beyond what was intended.

First, freedom of speech must be protected. When any person or entity holds power in society and uses that power to restrict the free expression of opinions and beliefs, we must pay attention and decide how we should vote in response. Suppose a law is passed that prohibits anyone speaking against a certain policy. Those who feel strongly for the policy will be pleased. But as a citizen-ruler, they should resist such a law because they know it violates the principle of free speech. Furthermore, understanding power, they know that some future government may use that same power to prohibit speech in the other direction.

Another example is a law that prohibits people in Group A from saying they believe that actions by people in Group B are wrong, immoral, or dangerous. Freedom of speech, which is essential to a free society, is fundamentally about the right to express dissenting views. Therefore, as an essential principle, citizen-rulers should refuse such laws. In addition to principle, a wise citizen-ruler knows that granting that power to the government or any other entity will eventually result in that power being used against other groups in unintended ways.

Every group should defend the right of other groups to express their views and assessments. Imagine we have two groups, Side A and Side B, who strongly oppose each other. Today, it is too common for both sides to try to silence or condemn the other. If instead citizens from both groups defended the rights of the other group to openly disagree in word and action, this would be a beginning step in promoting trust, compromise, and hope.

The second behavior deals with suppression and distortion of information. Government may use its power for those purposes. In some cases, however, these actions take place as an abuse of power outside of government. That is, those in power decide to suppress, distort, and deceive in order to influence public policy. This was discussed in detail in the "Information Structure" chapter. When citizens see any entity or individual, public or private, engaged in this behavior, they can look for ways to resist it by voting. It might be voting politically but more often it will be voting economically and socially.

The third behavior has to do with coercion in which political or economic power is used to coerce others to be quiet, act in ways that compromise or violate their values, or actively support policies that favor one group but violate the values of a second group. Coercion is sometimes used in the two behaviors discussed above. But coercion is increasingly going further and involves the direct threat of criminal or civil action in order to force behaviors. Here, Group A feels so strongly about a specific policy—that it is so good or right or just—it believes principles of freedom should be abandoned and that others should be forced to comply, even if that means punishing Group B or forcing them to act in violation of what they believe is good or right or just.

Using power to coerce others is extremely dangerous for a free society. It can quickly escalate social tensions beyond recovery. Thus, citizen-rulers must be vigilant and act quickly to eliminate it.

Coercion is on the rise today for several reasons. Citizens are giving up on persuasion. The political system is in stalemate. One group fears another group and sees the only way to protect themselves is to "defeat" the other group. A sense of urgency exists that demands "doing something," even if it damages freedom and coerces others.

Citizen-rulers must remember that coercion in any form is incompatible with a free society and that the power to coerce in one direction today will be used to coerce in the other direction tomorrow. Therefore, citizen-rulers on Side A should be looking for ways to reduce the sense of threat and coercion felt by Side B. No single behavior would be more effective and act more swiftly than if all citizen-rulers worked to remove threat and coercion.

When enough citizens in the middle part of the political spectrum begin addressing the above three behaviors, the social and political environment will steadily move toward the hope of cooperation, trust, and genuine compromise. At some point in this process, new potential political leaders may emerge, leaders who want to be elected on the basis of "reaching across the aisle." This rarely happens now because we as citizens have sent no signals indicating that is what we really want. When we do our part, when a sense of "we" begins replacing "us against them," potential leaders will respond accordingly.

What we have covered so far in this chapter are the essentials, those things that must come first in order to build the foundation for further progress. To restore those three behaviors will require adjustments to our mindset and perspective. Competing worldviews is not a problem to be solved by one worldview defeating another. The simultaneous presence of multiple, fundamental conceptions of the world is something we must learn to accept. Rather than trying to solve a problem that is not actually a problem at all, we should think in terms of process and perspective. This is comparable to what we learned about specific social problems: they cannot be solved in isolation or by treating symptoms. Instead, we must fix fundamental causes of those problems.

The divergence of our worldviews over the past five decades means that some citizens will hold elements of their worldview that contradict those held by others. For illustration, consider a few major examples. Some people believe in God, others do not. In both of those groups are people who believe strongly that life in society should be shaped by their particular beliefs. Some people believe that the economy should operate freely, with personal responsibility and rewards. Such an arrangement produces material prosperity but at the cost of social stress. Others believe society is better with less material prosperity and less intense economic activity. Some people believe that climate change is an impending catastrophe while others believe it is a modest long-term risk. Some believe that peace, freedom, and prosperity are now built into how the world operates. Others view those as achievements that are easily lost if not carefully cultivated.

What happens when one group believes that a certain issue, a certain element of a worldview, is so important that it poses an existential threat to society and, furthermore, that only their view of the issue can prevent collapse? At that point, society faces a critical junction where it will be difficult to continue supporting free speech, the facing of reality, and avoidance of coercion. If the group that believes the very existence of our society is under threat has sufficient power, it may be tempted to suspend the freedoms of opposing groups, and to feel completely justified in doing so. However, if two points are remembered, the temptation can be resisted. First, the group wishing to prevail may in fact be wrong. But even if their view is correct, there is almost certainly a way forward that does not involve coercion. Second, abandoning freedom and relying on coercion of other citizens is far more likely to bring about the collapse of society than is any specific problem, no matter how important it may appear.

It seems to me that in the last ten to fifteen years, it has become more common for groups to approach the limit at which they perceive an existential threat to society. I think this increased frequency is another symptom of growing anomie.

Stated simply, our reality is that we must deal with competing worldviews, even when elements of worldviews may be directly opposite each other. An attitude of "winning" must be replaced by a process of finding common ground, developing genuine tolerance, being willing to honestly compromise, and above all protecting and enhancing the three behaviors discussed above. As a society, we may need to be willing to conduct experiments. But any experiments involving elements of worldviews must be carried out carefully and slowly. Furthermore, they must be conducted with personal responsibility and undistorted feedback. These are the subject of the next chapter.

RESPONSIBILITY AND FEEDBACK

"Freedom is not fun. It is not the same as individual happiness, nor is it security or peace and progress. . . . But the essence of freedom lies elsewhere. It is responsible choice. It is not so much a right as a duty. . . . Unless there are decision and responsibility there is no freedom."
Peter Drucker

". . . and there is no possible compromise with an unsound theory; nature always steps in and exacts her penalty. Ignorance is no excuse with her; good intentions are no extenuation."
Albert Jay Nock

For our actions to be effective we must learn, and to learn we must have useful feedback. To know whether we should act and to shape how we act, we must know our responsibility. For each situation, for each domain of action, we must have a proper understanding of action-reaction, cause-effect, and behavior-consequence. In the natural realm, for example, gravity, it is easy to have proper understanding. The feedback is one way, from nature to us. We don't provide feedback to gravity. Furthermore, the feedback is perfectly consistent and immediate: we let go of an apple and it drops.

Of course, in the social realm, everything is different. We receive feedback, and we give feedback. We must have proper understanding for both directions. Our responsibility can be more difficult to ascertain. A central metaphor in this book is owners of a company finally understanding that their company is not profitable and is in danger of going out of business. This realization brings sharply into focus our responsibility as citizen-rulers. One of the many reasons we lost that focus is the idea from the middle of last century that society could be managed in a "scientific" manner. The assumption was that the various feedback signals in society could be understood and controlled in ways approximating what had been accomplished in the natural world.

As we've seen throughout this book, such assumptions were never justified. We can trace the causes of many of our problems back to those assumptions. Human action in society is not at all like the natural world. What happens in society is that the result of a particular action is not perfectly consistent nor does the result necessarily come about in the immediate future. A modern social system is complex, adaptive, and operates over long timeframes, sometimes decades. It is not at all like the natural world of our daily experience or the complicated mechanical and chemical devices created through engineering. In the absence of such certainty, we must order social life using fundamental principles together with careful analyses of our particular time and circumstances.

In our free society, acting as citizen-rulers, we now know that we assume more responsibility for understanding the feedback that comes to us and for giving feedback to others in society, most notably those with political, economic, and social power. In fact, as citizens we hold the ultimate power, or at least the potential for power. By our political, economic, and social votes we largely determine the well-being of our society in each of those domains. In earlier chapters we've discussed principles and analyses for the purpose of a proper understanding of causes, effects, responsibilities, and social feedback in general.

What we've covered so far enables us to be more intentional and cast better votes in our newly-assumed role as citizen-rulers. We've learned much about understanding causes and feedback, specifically how easy it is for feedback to become distorted or even removed. As a result, we are better equipped to continually improve the direction of our society by our votes. That is, we are much better informed about how to act "going forward."

However, there is one fundamental force that is so complicated and difficult to grasp that we must invest more effort to understand how to deal with it in the years ahead. That force comes from our monetary system and the power and financial structures based on it. While we as citizen-rulers can make a great difference in our society by our everyday votes as summarized above, we can't truly solve most of our problems without moderating this force.

In earlier chapters, we often noted the monetary system's connection to specific problems and how it distorted feedback and mitigated or delayed the true cost of policies and social actions. Our monetary system has enabled a tremendous concentration of power in the federal government, government in general, the financial industry, and large corporations. Our economic and social structures today are much different than they would have been under other monetary systems. Most of our major problems would not have progressed to their current state because the feedback signal of real costs—not concealed by monetary policies—would have generated corrective action long ago.

In the "Analysis and Synthesis" part of the book, we used the gold society as a reference point, a society that uses gold coins as their money. Such a system is directly opposite what we have today. In the former, additional money can be added to society only with effort whereas today money can be created instantaneously and with zero effort. To be clear, using gold coins as an example was not to imply that we can change our current monetary system to a gold coin society. The gold reference point was simply to emphasize how much differently society would operate. Every economic and political decision would have been weighed against its true cost, a cost that would have been made evident much sooner because it could not be hidden by debt and money creation.

Because the world's social, economic, and geopolitical structures are built upon our monetary system it will only change its essential foundations under some crisis. Therefore, the task of citizen-rulers is to vote in ways that reduce the undesirable effects of our present system.

Our first task—and it will be an ongoing task—is to unlearn what we've been (implicitly) taught for more than half a century, which is that monetary policy is a tool for government to solve problems, create economic growth, and create a better society. Looking back, we can see that reality is just the opposite. Our monetary and financial structure has enabled or caused many of the problems we face today. When money can be created out of nothing, it concentrates power and distorts signals within the economy and society.

While the mechanics and machinations of our monetary and financial structure are complicated and often intentionally obscure, the average citizen does not need that level of understanding. Many citizens with no training whatsoever in economics, finance, or banking nonetheless intuitively know that there is something wrong or dangerous about the power to create money and debt at will. They understand that those who have the power to create money will use that power for the advantage of some and disadvantage of all others.

This will be a hard lesson to learn. At the time of this writing, some leaders in government are wanting to double down on the use of monetary policy. For many decades, the Federal Reserve was authorized to act to control inflation and achieve full employment. Now, there is talk of adding two additional mandates to the federal reserve. One is to support climate policy, and the other is to promote racial equity. Of course, all citizens want low inflation, employment, a healthy climate, and freedom for all citizens regardless of race. However, the lessons from the last 70 years teach us that monetary policy should be made more neutral, not more influential. The goals of society should be created and enacted through the legislative process and funded in honest, understandable ways.

As is true for all of our specialized domains, whether medical care, education, or criminal justice, we need citizens who are willing to learn in detail about our monetary and financial structure. In each of these domains, citizens can find trusted sources as discussed earlier.

It is well beyond the scope of this book to attempt detailed recommendations for how to understand and vote in the area of monetary policy. Nonetheless, based on fundamental principles and analyses presented earlier, some broad guidance is possible.

The single most powerful change that would minimize the distortions of monetary policy would be a requirement for the federal government to operate with a balanced budget. The second most powerful, and probably a necessary part of the first, is to change the mandate of the Federal Reserve so that its only job is to ensure the integrity of the banking system, not to control inflation or drive employment. These major changes are unlikely in the near term. Fortunately, however, they are not prerequisites for progress. There are still ways for citizens to vote to minimize the impact of monetary policy.

We as a society run a federal government with a budget deficit because we ask more of government than we are willing to fund by increased taxes. Some of this asking is implicit; we want government to mitigate the symptoms of problems rather than addressing their causes. As we resume our role of citizen-ruler, we can vote against legislation that spends money to address symptoms. We can vote against legislation that discourages personal responsibility. We can vote for legislation that addresses fundamental causes and encourages personal responsibility, which as it turns out tends to cost far less money than the former policies. Because we don't vote directly on federal legislation, our votes will be for and against particular politicians.

We can support policies and initiatives that tend to reduce the power of the federal government, the finance industry, and extremely large corporations. This is not because those institutions or the people within them are intrinsically bad or have the intent to harm. It is because concentrated power is inherently dangerous. The benefits of concentrated power must be carefully weighed against those dangers. At this point in our society, the harm and danger exceed the benefits. Therefore, a new balance needs to be applied. Here, we must be careful lest we fall into a trap. Asking the federal government to adjust the balance of power either for itself or for any other domain will ultimately increase the power of not only the government but the domains they are supposedly rebalancing. To reduce the level of concentration of power will require politicians willing to support legislation that fundamentally changes the rules.

Finally, we consider the feedback of citizens based on how we assess and select our elected leaders. To begin, we remember a basic premise of this book: our current state of affairs, our current political situation, and most anything else we can think of is the result of the collective political, economic, and social votes of citizens.

When we look for causes, when we want to cast blame, we must look in the mirror.

Earlier in the book, we talked about casting all of our types of voting with the principle of "self-interest properly understood" always in view. When it comes to electing our government leaders, additional considerations come into play. Personal character, integrity, relevant experience, and demonstrated proper understanding should take precedence over support for some single favorite issue. Those characteristics should also take precedence over charisma. Returning to our metaphor of owners resuming control of their company, we are looking for trustworthy and competent people to govern our society for the success of everyone. These characteristics are frequently talked about and frequently touted, but if all citizens were making such assessments a priority and making the assessments wisely, would we have our current political climate?

Another aspect of assessing potential political leaders is less discussed than the characteristics above. It has long been recognized that democracies tend to take a short view rather than a long view. We want answers and we want them now. Furthermore, we make our assessments almost totally based on short-term outcomes rather than on the processes that were used to arrive at decisions and policies. Certainly, outcomes are important and should be one of the criteria in assessments. But short-term outcomes are overweighted by many citizens when voting. Part of the reason is human nature: more people tend to have a short-term view than a long-term view.

But the more important reason likely comes from the implicit bargain discussed earlier in the book. If we have come to believe that society can be managed according to universal laws analogous to the laws of physics, we will reasonably expect quick and certain results. If we are not quite that deterministic in our views but nonetheless believe that society can be managed as a business, we will still expect relatively short-term, and relatively certain outcomes. At a minimum, those models failed to account for luck and unexpected events. A company that is managed with excellence may still suffer for a long time due to events outside of its control or that could not have been reasonably planned for.

The functioning of a society is far more complex than that of an organization. None of the important elements of society are subject to anything like the regularity and certainty of natural laws. Nor does society function like a well-run company. Each individual in a free society will respond in uniquely adaptive ways to the actions of every other person and entity within society. It cannot be predicted. This reality was effectively overlooked in the implicit bargain. Thus, as a society we tended to expect fast and certain results.

Those who sought political power quickly learned how to adjust to those expectations. Politicians who attempted to explain their thinking and their methods, or changed their minds based on new understanding, tended to be rejected by voters. The lesson was easily learned. Politicians learned their chances for election were better if they avoided responsibility, created "spin" on every event and outcome, and avoided admitting to a change in thinking or position. Is that what we as citizen-rulers really want for those we elect to help run society? Would we not be better served by people who think carefully, explain their thinking and methods, and operate according to fundamental principles and public analyses? If so, then our assessments should be based on those things rather than on a specific result.

Perhaps most importantly, if we as citizens understand that society cannot be managed to produce specific outcomes, that politicians cannot guarantee prosperity and a good life, we will support leaders who operate on fundamental principles. We will do so because we understand that our best chance for peace, prosperity, and a good life come not from specific government policies but from a truly free society—with its attendant responsibilities.

TRANSITION

"When will there be justice in Athens? There will be justice in Athens when those who are not injured are as outraged as those who are."
Thucydides

"Injustice anywhere is a threat to justice everywhere."
Martin Luther King Jr.

As more citizens increasingly assume the role of citizen-ruler, changes will begin to happen. As we gain proper understanding and put into action ideas discussed earlier, we can expect two initial stages of change. First, when the threat of coercion is replaced by a desire for persuasion and cooperation, the political and social climate will improve. As we learn to accept the reality of worldviews with competing elements and commit ourselves as a society to learn how to live well together, social tension will gradually decline. We can even hope for the state of anomie to slowly subside.

At some point, the first stage will have progressed far enough and its effects spread wide enough to have produced a climate in which positive change can be discussed. Neither of these stages can be rushed or forced. These stages can be expedited if people who already hold power join the movement—truly join, not attempt to use it as yet another means to keep and increase power. The stages will also be expedited as new leaders exhibit credibility in proper understanding and a willingness to lead in accordance with fundamental principles and honest analysis.

What should we expect during this time of transition? Most importantly, it will not be smooth and easy. Even if many citizens commit themselves to proper understanding, there will be many disagreements. Understanding fundamental principles and good analyses is the first step, but it doesn't mean that everyone will agree on priorities or courses of action. It is critically important that during those times of disagreement we do not slide backward into coercion and a rush for power at all costs. A large majority of citizens, by observing what is taking place in all of society, must develop confidence in the new approach. Given the political, social, and economic backdrop of the past twenty years, we should expect this confidence-building to be a slow process.

How can we assess progress in the creation of this new political and social climate? Perhaps the best indicator will be when citizens who previously were on different sides of the political dividing line begin making an honest attempt to understand each other and find common ground. This also will take time because those individuals and groups must build trust, and trust is built slowly.

All along the way, these movements to eliminate coercion, encourage persuasion and cooperation, and to work across the dividing line will be met by resistance and sabotage from groups who are threatened by the new approach. Those on the extremes of the political spectrum, both left and right, will resist the movement because they are committed not to cooperation and a harmonious society but to an absolute subduing of those on the other extreme.

Resistance will also come from individuals and groups who are not part of the extreme but who realize their positions of power and favor cannot survive in a society that operates in the spirit of cooperation and compromise or in conformity with fundamental principles and honest analyses. These groups may be the most dangerous. It is easy enough to recognize the extremes on either end of the political spectrum. However, those closer to the middle who feel threatened are more likely to cloak themselves as supporters of the new approach while in fact working to sabotage it so that the status quo may remain. Fortunately, it will not be difficult to identify those actions and groups when properly and honestly analyzed.

We will need patience during this time because it may seem as if nothing is happening. As a society, we will be breaking our habitual expectation that "somebody should do something." As a society, we will need a time of calm, of not pressing for "solutions," of resisting the urge to force others to conform to our desires. Only in a period of calm can we develop new ways of interacting and increasing levels of trust.

Though it may not be obvious, additional important and valuable changes will be happening on our way to building a critical mass of citizen-rulers capable of working together. We will be conditioning ourselves to think and act in light of fundamental principles and careful analyses. As more citizens realize their actions are votes that influence society, whether politically, economically, or socially, it will have a forming influence upon all citizens. This ongoing, gradual shift in the understanding and perspective of citizens is an essential precursor to future policies directed at the fundamental causes of our pressing problems.

Eventually, critical mass will be achieved: truly effective changes in policies and structure will become possible. We will need caution. For example, imagine that the transitional changes are phenomenally successful. The new "middle group" might be so encouraged and enthused by their potential for working together that they slip into the old way of thinking, which might result in trying to coerce change in those closer to the fringes. Instead, the approach to concrete changes should be preceded by explanations that tie back to fundamental principles and careful analyses. As much as possible, every citizen should be convinced that a proposed action is fair and just. The time required for persuasion and compromise may be longer than the old method of coercion, but the effort invested will pay off in terms of true solutions.

Another caution: because political stalemate will have been broken, it would be easy to fall back into the decades-long mindset of trying to solve problems individually and to make such attempts starting from the symptoms of the problem rather than from the fundamental causes. The old mindset might try to address family life, education, medical care, economic inequality, criminal justice, and so on by policies specific to those domains. While some such specific policies will of course be required, the first step toward solutions must look at the fundamental causes shared by all of them. Those fundamental causes, discussed throughout the book, can be broadly captured in two concepts: (1) personal responsibility, (2) restoring honest feedback.

When the time comes for particular policies, part of the assessment of whether they are fair will be based on the timeframe over which they will be implemented and how the costs and adjustments are allocated. For illustration, consider Social Security and Medicare. As discussed in an earlier chapter, these programs are facing a funding problem over the next several years. Because these are long-standing "social contract" programs on which many people have planned the last decades of their lives, any changes that have a chance of being judged as fair will have to be implemented over a couple of decades. A citizen who is already receiving those benefits should not feel threatened about the remaining years of their support. Similarly, we probably can't change the rules of the game on someone who is 55 years old. Ten years would not be sufficient time for them to make adjustments. On the funding side, younger citizens who have many years of their working life ahead of them may have to pay higher taxes as their contribution to bring the system into balance. The key point is all citizens will be required to work together in order to find a fair and just solution.

Other problems may only be considered fair and just if they are implemented over a short period of time and with a heavy emphasis on responsibility and adjustment at the individual level. For example, if there are currently working-age people capable of working who instead are being supported by their taxpaying fellow citizens, the fair and just thing might be to impose personal responsibility quickly.

We, citizens of our time, might legitimately claim that it is unfair that the problems and deferred costs of previous generations fall on our generation and perhaps on that of our children. Such a claim could be argued in different ways. In any event, our reality must be accepted and dealt with as fairly and justly as possible.

CONCLUSION

"... you will understand that, of all governments, the government of democracy, despite its flaws, is still the most appropriate to make this society prosper."
Alexis de Tocqueville

"If man is not to do more harm than good in his efforts to improve the social order, he will have to learn that in this, as in all other fields where essential complexity of an organized kind prevails, he cannot acquire the full knowledge which would make mastery of the events possible. He will therefore have to use what knowledge he can achieve, not to shape the results as the craftsman shapes his handiwork, but rather to cultivate a growth by providing the appropriate environment, in the manner in which the gardener does this for his plants."
F. A. Hayek

We opened this book by stating that when things are not working and when attempted solutions only make the problems worse, it is time to stop. It is time to work backward and find critical junctions from which we work forward again, reframing the problem built upon better understanding. This book is dedicated to that project.

We acknowledged that our problems are indeed serious, and we should address them with urgency. However, our approach to solutions has to be completely different than what we've attempted for decades. Our society is approaching a point of crisis. The extent of contention, disagreement, hardening of positions, and willingness to coerce others is on a trajectory that threatens our society.

I proposed two essential keys for finding our way forward. What must come first is a recognition that all of our problems and all of our structures exist today because of the votes cast by "we the people," that is, those who are alive and voting today as well as those who are no longer with us. We do not vote under physical threat. We are truly free to cast our political, economic, and social votes. Thus, complaints about the economy, the political figures in Washington we see as incompetent, the breakdown of families, and so on must all be directed back to us as citizens.

Having taken the first step of accepting our responsibility as citizens, the second key is a commitment to gain proper understanding so we can reframe our problems in ways that allow them to be solved. This is different than the way we currently frame them, a way which makes them intractable. Our urgency, therefore, is to understand and address basic challenges in society; it is not an urgency to "do something."

Stated succinctly, we the people must be willing to accept our role as citizens-rulers and to do so with a larger investment of time and attention toward proper understanding.

Because government, especially the federal government, has acquired so much power, we tend to focus most of our attention and voting on what takes place in the voting booth. Certainly, our political votes are crucial, but our collective economic and social votes are just as important because we cast them multiple times every day. Our ongoing economic and social voting shapes society on a continuous basis as many millions of citizens vote multiple times a day.

As a useful reference point, I selected 1950 to mark the new world order and social order that emerged following the tumultuous first half of last century that ended with World War II. It is hard to overstate the depth and scope of differences that came about throughout the world in the 50 years from 1900 to 1950. We looked at many of these differences as we attempted to understand not just what happened but how it could have happened and how it transpired.

Some of the most important consequences of those changes can be captured in a few concepts. The United States emerged from the first half of the century as the preeminent world power militarily, economically, and socially. Our capacity for action both on the world stage and as individuals within our society increased rapidly. We had high confidence in science and in the idea that society could be scientifically managed by government. Thus, an "implicit bargain" formed in which citizens handed off the management of all aspects of our society to chosen elites.

Over the next 50 years, changing worldviews and changing demographics weakened or removed some of the traditional sources of authority and some of the institutions and environments that previously formed the next generation of citizens. By the start of the twenty-first century, worldviews had diverged so much that some elements were in competition. That is, some citizens valued things opposed by other citizens. Further, for many citizens, the important forming institutions of family and education were in disarray. The influence of organized, traditional religion was far less than any other time in American history—though religion properly understood was as powerful as ever.

We could say we outran ourselves. Our *capacity* for action increased rapidly while our traditional foundations for knowing what we *should* be doing were declining, with no replacements in sight.

The first decade of the new century made clear that society could not be managed by "scientific" methods and that the implicit bargain had failed. Not just in the United States, but in other countries also, citizens responded with surprising political "rebellions." In response, some elites decided to restrict freedom of speech and use their power to control and shape those citizens who were "rebelling." What had been forming for decades suddenly became unavoidably clear. Our problems and our dissension are worse than we had recognized (or admitted). The elite leadership have no ideas for true solutions. The only ideas are the old ones: spend money, increase power and control. Yet our problems not only remain, they are worsening.

We are stuck and therefore must do the hard work of figuring out what happened.

We learn by acting, then observing the results of our actions, and then making adjustments based on whether our objectives were achieved. Throughout the book, we've talked about this feedback process. One of our first questions must therefore be, what happened to that process? Why did the learning loop fail?

That question was studied throughout the book. While there are many parts to the answer, they can be summarized in a couple of broad categories. First, our changing worldviews and the implicit bargain predisposed us to not recognize some of the feedback signals. But that alone would not have negated the process for long. What enabled the decades of missing, distorted, or ignored feedback signals were two characteristics unique to the United States. One of those was sustained economic growth for decades. However, the critical characteristic was that the United States owned the world's monetary system. Those two characteristics, working together, enabled the United States to borrow heavily and create money that was used for policies and programs that hampered the feedback process.

Distorted feedback and improper understanding inhibit learning. If we don't learn, we don't make adjustments. The consequences of that broken process depend upon the particular system in question, something we looked at in the chapter dedicated to feedback. When the system of concern is society, the consequences can be captured in two broad categories. First, society will develop distorted structures that tend to hold onto the problems. Second, the costs associated with unlearned lessons will be hidden, postponed for some later day of reckoning.

As it turns out, that day is today. We must not only work out how to pay the bills now coming due, we must develop proper understanding so that we can make good decisions going forward. We need to redefine the roles and responsibilities within society generally and in governance specifically. Our social structures need adjustments. We have problems to address. All of this must be taken on after we learn what is necessary in our role as true citizen-rulers.

A society functions as a complex adaptive system, not as a mechanistic and deterministic system. Yet, it is the latter characteristics that must be present if something is to be "scientifically" managed. In a complex adaptive system, it is impossible to consistently predict what will happen, and it is outright impossible to control what will happen.

When we operate, and our government operates, as if society is mechanistic and deterministic, the approach is to pass law after law and regulation after regulation to obtain the desired outcomes. Under our fiat monetary system, we can add to rules and regulations the attempt to control the economy and behavior by monetary and fiscal policy. But decades of experience have proved that those in power make use of such methods of control to further concentrate their power. This concentration works to the advantage of those in power and to the disadvantage of the remainder of citizens.

Furthermore, those methods of control tend to hide, distort, and postpone feedback signals that would have brought about corrective behavior.

When we understand society as a complex adaptive system and when we see the results produced by the methods and policies used by government since 1950, it becomes clear why we must return to fundamental principles. Only by understanding and conforming to such principles can we hope to influence the direction of society—influence, not control. Our efforts will only be successful if those fundamental principles are applied with careful and honest analysis and synthesis. In this new approach, we must abandon the idea that we as citizens of a free society can specify exactly what we want to happen and exactly how it can be made to happen. Instead, our perspective must first shift to establishing and protecting the proper social environment and second to ensuring honest feedback by which individual citizens can assume personal responsibility.

As we resume our role as citizen-rulers, we will pay more attention to the governance of our society than was assumed necessary under the "implicit bargain." We will invest more time and effort to develop proper understanding so that all of our votes (political, economic, social) shape society for continued freedom, prosperity, and peace. A natural result of this change in perspective and functioning will be to mitigate the concept of "the government" as something separate from the citizenry. Whatever is called "the government" is there because we as citizens have created and allowed it.

In an earlier part of the book, we analyzed several important structures in our society. A proper understanding of those structures and how they operate is essential for a citizen-ruler. Each citizen should have some knowledge of those structures. However, we will usually rely on "trusted sources" as discussed in an earlier chapter for in-depth understanding.

A critical clarification is required regarding structures. At the time of this writing, several groups are promoting the idea that structures are the problem, that the structures themselves possess bias, racism, suppression, or other evils. From that mindset, those groups suppose that the structures themselves can be fixed directly. In extreme cases, people advocate for the structures to be destroyed. Because the starting analysis is incorrect, so is the proposed solution.

Structures, like government, exist because they were created and allowed by citizens. An attempt to "fix" a structure directly is an example of treating symptoms rather than causes. Structures, both their creation and maintenance, result from the cumulative political, economic, and social votes of the citizenry. Those elements of a structure that are not working as we would like must be addressed fundamentally. Enough individual citizens must gain proper understanding and cast their votes accordingly such that the structures undergo adjustment—driven by the votes of citizens informed by principles and honest analyses.

Therefore, we study structures in order to understand what we built and how things work at present. But in a free society, change begins with individual citizens. As citizen-rulers gain proper understanding, they will be motivated to change their behavior and their votes. Out of those personal changes will come adjustments to existing structures.

Some might argue that not enough citizens are motivated to take on the role of citizen-ruler. If that is true, it is because the feedback-adjustment process has been broken for decades. Stated differently, the true costs and consequences of actions have not been manifest. Throughout the book, I've tried to make the case that this is soon going to change. The costs and consequences will increasingly become painful. I've encouraged us to begin now acquiring proper understanding of what has happened, why it has happened, and what we can do going forward.

Fortunately, we do not have to create some new, magical way to bring about the feedback-adjustment process. The way the world works, the natural laws of the world, inherently give feedback. Only in the last 70 years have the circumstances of our society been such that we could distort, hide, or postpone costs and consequences—albeit only temporarily. Thus, our task is not to create something new; it is to identify and remove what interferes with the feedback-adjustment process.

As we've discussed throughout the book, multiple factors contribute to the brokenness of that process. However, only one thing has enabled the process to remain broken for so long: our monetary system. If each citizen at each point in time over the past 70 years had (1) to pay the then-current costs for their actions and those of other citizens, and (2) understood what costs and consequences they were deferring to their children, I believe the process would have adjusted long ago. Thus, it is essential that we (1) reform our monetary system as much as we can, and (2) more importantly, conduct fiscal and monetary policy as if the system were already reformed.

Over the next couple of decades we face difficult decisions and hard effort as we address our problems. However, we have many reasons for optimism. While we certainly face high levels of divisiveness and discord at present, I believe they do not run as wide and deep as they may appear. I believe a large majority of Americans on either side of the political dividing line share many values. When that large majority decide to work together based on shared values and agree to avoid trying to coerce others to agree with them about differing values, we can quickly begin making progress. We have strong institutions of government. The same is true of private organizations, both profit and nonprofit. Our infrastructure, both physical and soft, is pervasive and strong. The structures that exist in society hold much that is good and strong. We can build on those things as we make adjustments and corrections.

Freedom, prosperity, and peace are not natural. It is difficult to produce the circumstances in which they are possible. It is also difficult to invest the constant effort required to protect and maintain them. While it is true that on our current path those goods are threatened, the desire for them runs deep among most Americans. As we develop proper understanding as citizen-rulers, we will recognize the threats and be prepared to do what is required to restore, protect, and maintain freedom, prosperity, and peace. In all of our work that lies ahead, we will remember that much depends on "self-interest properly understood."

ACKNOWLEDGEMENTS

I could not have written this book without the work of many who preceded me. My book is reliant on, and I am indebted to, a multitude of thinkers and leaders who, over centuries, developed insights, concepts, and foundations which I lack the capacity to produce no matter how much time I might have been given.

For my parents, I am deeply thankful. It is a great blessing, and a head start in life to be raised in a good home and to be trained in the ways of a citizen.

Steve Jordan, who was first my boss and then for decades my business partner—and always a friend—was instrumental in shaping my understanding of the world. He had confidence in me before I had yet earned it. I very much appreciate his influence.

Chris Andersen, my longtime friend and business partner, has been a source of ideas and refinement for my thinking. He suffered through some of my early draft writing. I am thankful for his friendship and his contribution to my development.

For my brothers, Bruce and Greg, and my friend Todd Craig, I am thankful for their work-in-progress review. For Greg's willingness to endure a review of an early version as well as the current manuscript, I am especially grateful.

I especially thank Selena Holland, who, in the final stages of the project, stepped in to help polish and refine the manuscript.

I was fortunate to work with 1106 Design through the publishing process. Their expertise and support are much appreciated.

Most importantly, over the past couple of decades, my wife Carolyn has been steadfast in her support, patience, and encouragement during the many hours every week devoted to this project. In addition, during the writing process, she reviewed and edited my drafts. Without her love, faith, and support, I would not have completed this book. I am deeply and forever grateful for her as my life partner.

INDEX

A
Age of Reason, 33, 34
anomie, 2, 141–144, 160, 178, 248, 255, 267

B
balanced budget, 261
banking system, 149–150, 153–158
Bastiat, Frederick, 230
belief systems
    centrality of, 15, 247–248
    present characteristics of, 76–79
    principles of, 73–76
bell curve, 14–15, 75
benefit scales, 23–24
Bill of Rights, 65
Bretton Woods Agreement, 150–151

C
"cancelling," 110, 140
capitalism, 108, 192, 224–225, 227–228, 232
Catholic Church, 77
character, 198, 204
Chavez, Hugo, 95–96
Christianity, 33–34, 74–78, 133–144, 173, 187, 248
citizens as rulers, 5–6, 83–88, 101, 111–113, 119, 168, 230, 239–244, 249, 251–253, 258–260, 264, 269, 274, 277–279, 281
Clinton, Hillary, 140
coercion, 248, 267–270
"college problem," 206–210, 220
communism, 35–36, 44, 77
companies, growth in size, 43
concern, in scientific management of society, 170
conflict, 15–16
Confucianism, 74–75
Constitution, US, 65, 66
contribution, 198, 204
conversion to belief system, 75–76
coronavirus pandemic, 190
credibility, breakdown in perception of, 105–106, 140–141
culture, 198, 204

D
de Tocqueville, Alexis, 7
debt, 42, 151–154, 158, 159, 162–163
"defund the police," 140

democracy
  communism vs., 35–36
  defined, 64–65
  equality and, 172–175
  limits on power in, 71
  meaning of term, 107–108
  modern, 167–179
  rulership structure and, 168–169
Democracy in America, 7
demographics, 126–128, 201–203
disruption, 43, 51
distortion, 89–90, 92–94, 96–98, 117
division of labor, 124–125
divisiveness, polarization, 68–69, 249–251, 268, 270, 280–281
"do something" solutions, 237–245
Durkheim, Emile, 141–142

E
economic freedom, 172, 185, 228
economic growth, 122–124
economics
  current state of, 115–117
  defined, 38
  division of labor and, 124–125
  education and, 202
  fairness of present economic system, 228
  full employment economy and, 35
  fundamental principles of, 37–40
  government management of economy, 192
  knowledge, tools, and science (KTS) and, 51–53
  need for new understanding of, 223
  overview of systems, 224–226
  present characteristics of system, 40–45, 226–228
  prices and, 118–119
  production and, 118–119
  relation to government, religion, 60
  scientific management of society, post-WWII, 67–70
  specialization and, 124–126
education
  current state of, 203–210
  history of US, 199–203
  preparation milieu and, 203–212, 218–219, 226
  social purposes of, 197–199
  solution framework for, 210–221
effectiveness, in human action, 25–26
employment, Federal Reserve and, 261
ends and means, 22–24, 28, 135
equality, 172–174, 175, 176
"equality of outcomes," 173, 174, 212
equality under the law, 175–176, 177–178
exchange, 23, 25, 40
expectations, 184–190

F
fairness, 25, 175–176, 184–190, 187, 189, 193–194, 195, 212, 228
"fake news," 110
families, strengthening, 213
federal government, intervention into economy, 149–150, 152–153, 158–164, 178–179, 192, 230, 259–262, 277–278
Federal Reserve, 119, 150–152, 261
Federal Reserve Deposit Insurance Corporation (FDIC), 150
feedback-adjustment process, 31, 87, 89, 89–100, 137–138, 143, 195, 205, 257–265, 276–277, 280
fiat system, 151, 159–161, 162, 228–229, 260–261, 277–278
financial crisis of 2008, 45, 68–69, 139–140, 143–144, 152–153, 190, 192, 210, 227
financial system. see monetary system

fiscal policy, 280
free markets, 117, 224–226
free speech, 248, 251–252, 254, 276
freedom. see also economic freedom;
   conditions for, 281
   instrumental value of, 65
   license vs., 71
   in modern democracies, 171–173
   power and, 59–71
   as solution to economic problems, 239
   tenuous nature of, 62–63
full employment economy, 35

G

gold economy, 146–148, 153–157, 159, 160–161, 163, 259–260
government (rulership structures)
   citizens as rulers, 5–6, 83–88, 101, 111–113, 119, 168, 230, 239–244, 249, 251–253, 258–260, 264, 269, 277–279, 281
   control of by social groups, 248
   credibility of, 104–105
   democracy and, 64–65
   failure of, 5–7
   forming public opinion, behavior, 70
   knowledge, tools, and science (KTS) and, 52–56
   limitations on power of, 60–61
   modern democratic, 167–179
   perception of legitimacy, 61, 69–70
   relation to economy, 60
   religion and, 60
   scientific management of society, post-WWII, 67–70
   socialization of costs and, 172–175
government management of economy, 35, 38–45, 230
government spending, 160, 229
Great Depression, 35

Great Recession. see financial crisis of 2008
gross domestic product, 41

H

hard versus soft science, 51–53, 87
human action, 26–28
human nature
   basic principles of, 13–20
   justice and fairness and, 175–176
   monetary system and, 148
   social structure and, 137, 139

I

images, information quality and, 105–110
individuality, principle of action, 21–22
inequality
   capitalism and, 225
   causes of, 186–190, 195
   citizen responsibility for, 231–232
   debt and, 158
   fairness and, 184–190, 195
   feedback-adjustment process and, 164
   government creation of, 230–232
   importance of, 183–184
   misidentification of causes, 227
   nature of economic system and, 230–233
   preparation milieu and, 218–219
   proposed solutions to, 190–196
   solution framework for, 193–195
   unemployment, underemployment and, 128
inflation, 42, 151–152, 162–163, 261
information
   distortion, 248
   trust in, 239–244, 279
information structure
   control of information and, 108–113

use, meaning of words and, 106–108
volume, quality of information and, 103
Islam, 76, 77

J
justice, 175–176

K
knowledge, in scientific management of society, 170
knowledge, tools, and science (KTS)
   basic to humanity, 47
   bolstering political legitimacy and, 52–53
   economics and, 51–53
   failure to understand long-term consequences of science, 54
   government and, 52–56
   hard versus soft science, 51–53
   material well-being and, 48
   present characteristics of, 49–57
   principles of, 47–49
   resources required for, 49
   science as driver of rapid change, 53–54
   science's loss of credibility, 54–56
   scientism and, 56–57
   social disruption and, 50–51
   transformative nature of, 48–49
   unchanging nature of, 48
   worldview and, 48–50

L
leaders, political; assessing, 263
license, vs. freedom, 71

M
Maduro, Nicholas, 95
Marx, Karl, 44, 225
Maslow, Abraham, 27
Maslow's hierarchy, 22–23, 27, 38, 134–136, 142, 171

Medicare, 127, 270–271
monetary policy, 229, 231. see also monetary system
monetary system
   abuse by ruling class, 40
   current system, 152–165
   development of, 146–152
   federal government control over, 153, 227, 277–278, 280
   feedback-adjustment process and, 259–261, 276
   as fiat system, 151, 159–162, 228–229, 260–261, 277–278
   influence on human action, 28
   modern economic system and, 45
   power of, 145
moral codes, 15, 61

N
natural law, 61–62
"newness," 136
news media, perception of fairness in, 189

O
offshoring, 125–126

P
pattern-seeking, meaning-seeking behavior, 16, 19
pensions, underfunded, 127
personality, 14
persuasion, vs. coercion, 70, 267–270
Plutarch, 193
population growth, 31, 39, 41
positive law, 62
power, freedom and
   present characteristics of, 64–71
   principles of, 59–64
preparation milieu, 203–212, 218–219, 226
presidential election of 2016, 69, 70

Index

presidential election of 2020, 70–71, 140–141, 220, 223
price inflation of 2022, 190. see also inflation
prices, 118–119, 228–229, 230
primary, secondary sources of information, 241–244
private property, 224, 228, 232
production, 118–119
prosperity, 26–27, 33, 36, 39, 42, 52, 54, 64–65, 123–124, 135, 137, 171, 185–186, 223–224, 228, 254, 264, 281
psychology, 184

R

rationality, human action and, 24–25
Reagan, Ronald, 151
Reason, Cult of, 77
reason, vs. religion, 33–34
recessions, 227. see also financial crisis of 2008
redistribution, 191
regulation, government, 86, 192, 229, 277–278
relativism, 173–174
religion, 15, 18–19, 33–34, 60, 74, 76–79, 133–144, 187, 247–248, 275
reserve currency, 150–151
responsibility, 257–265
responsibility, as citizen-rulers, 274
retirement, 126–127, 189
Roosevelt, Franklin, 191–192

S

savings, 127, 159, 160
scarcity, 22
schooling, 200. see also education
science, 42, 50–53, 105, 140–141
scientific management of society, post-WWII, 34–36, 67–70, 83, 85–86, 139–140, 167–170, 203, 205, 237–238, 258, 263–264, 275–277, 278
scientism, 56–57, 77–78
self-correction, 92. see also feedback-adjustment process
social democracy, 44
social relations, economics and, 126–128
Social Security, 127, 270–271
social structure
    breakdown in, 129–144
    economics and, 159–165
    human nature and, 137, 139
socialism, 95–96, 108, 192, 224–226, 232
socialization of costs, 172–175
Soviet Union, 225
specialization, economic, 124–126, 185
standard of living, increasing, 27, 32, 39–42
"structures," seen as problematic, 279
subjectivism, 173–174
syncretism, 78

T

taxation, 227, 229, 230, 271
temperament, 14
tolerance, 140–141
trade, 40
transition, period of, 267–271
Trump, Donald, 68, 140
trust
    breakdown in, 57, 105–106, 130, 132–133, 241–243
    rebuilding, 243–244, 250, 252–253, 268–269, 279

U

unemployment, underemployment, 126–128
universal basic income (UBI), 191

V

variability, of natural traits, 14–19

Venezuela, 95–96, 225–226
videos, deceptive, 106
votes, citizen, 4–6, 66, 112, 117, 119,
  126, 195, 216–219, 229–231, 239–241,
  243, 258–263, 274–275, 278–279

W

"War on Poverty," 230
wisdom, 86
wisdom, in scientific management of
  society, 170
words, changes in use, meaning of,
  106–108
worldviews
  acceptance of differences in, 267
  changes in, 133–135
  competition among, 247–255,
    275–276
  defined, 29–30
  education and, 204
  equality under law and, 177–178
  fairness and, 187
  knowledge, tools, and science
    (KTS) and, 48–50
  present characteristics of, 31–36
  principles of, 29–31

Made in the USA
Monee, IL
01 June 2023